My lagos experience in Lagos

I was caught up with working out in my privately made exercise center at the backyard of my home in apapa Lagos when my mom called to me.. "Charlie!!!!....charlie ooooooo!!!!.....come and welcome your August guest ".

I wasn't expecting anybody, and I seldom had visitors. At first, I respected him and generally alluded to him as "August guest " (a title she gave for any preferred visitor). Be that as it may, my ex would prefer to pass on rather than see me. We headed out in different directions sharply and realizing him excessively well, he would prefer to be some place getting screwed for cash than reconciling for affection.

I immediately finished my weight training count and went to the lounge to meet whoever this individual was. As I got into the dinning room and took a sachet of water from the refrigerator, I could hear a profound baritone voice giggling from the parlor. I likewise heard a lady's voice which wasn't my moms.

Perspiring from my functioning out meeting and topless, I attempted to bring a peep into the front room to see who was visiting . Be that as it may, it was past the point of no return. I was seen right away. I was at that point yelling for bliss before my cerebrum completely enlisted the affirmation of who it perceived.

"chuzzziiieeeee!!!!!!" I continued to shout as I flew into his huge opened arms. Without

disapproving my sweat-soaked body , he embraced me back. More tight. He was currently taller and more greater in muscle . However couple of years more established than me , he looked very good...perhaps in light of the fact that life wasn't challenging for him.

Aunt bliss (his mom) who however was presently matured and dark very much like my mum, actually had her snappy class. She attempted to embrace me however was an extremely cautious about Not allowing my wet body to contact her white suit.

"wow!!!! Na you be this? It's been what???? Very nearly 20 years????" he said as he held me a decent foot separated featuring at me.

"you're no longer Mr ske" he prodded as he punched me on my chest.

I used to be thin as a youngster and was prodded alot about it. As a matter of fact I was called Skelton concerning the person in the famous animation "super ted" so they abbreviated the name to "ske".

Since I was prodded a ton, I went into working out. However I didn't collect a lot of mass, I was happy with my thin form.

Chizoba (chuzie) used to be my dearest companion in essential, junior and senior auxiliary school. We were near the point that our mom's wound up companions. We likewise went to similar church and on many events, my mom permitted me rest over at their home. It was during one of those rest overs that I had my most memorable same sex experience.

We had quite recently completed the process of watching wrestle madness and chose to evaluate some wrestling. He was around 17 and I was around 14. Since he was more grounded than me, he kept over controlling me. In wrestling, it was the practice to lie with on leg on each side of your adversary and build up to three preceding you were announced victor. So chuzie laid on me however rather than with on leg on each side of, he was opposite.

Instead of building up to 3, he continued to drag out the count. "oooneee.....one and a half, one, one quarter.....one a portion of a quarter ...."

I laid still and I could feel his pulsating dick on my stomach. I also was hard. As he counted, I just featured at him. "what?" he asked me with a little dislike his face. "what's going on with everything?" I asked in kind . Going after my dick, he said "this". As he contacted it, his eyes became wide with suprise. Particularly early on, my dick was at that point a very long time in front of me. To be sure my thin height was all around redressed.

I was so amazed when he removed his shorts as though they were ablaze , spat in his grasp and started stroking my dick. Considering it now , it is obvious he was at that point physically dynamic particularly early on.

I just laid there like a faker as he stroked me. Sooner or later he went on me and started sucking my dick. He got up spat on all fours it in his rooster. Spat once more and focused on it his butt. He sat across me and situated my dick which was currently peeping from the edge of my shorts in complete focus into his opening. He continued to stroke his dick and drops of precum arrived on my belly.

Gradually he started going down on me as he wanked himself. He was just most of the way when I felt hot consuming vibe that sent warms of enthusiasm flooding through my veins. I started to shake as I shot a ludicrous measure of cum straight into his butt.

His eyes was still close as he wanked his chicken quicker. Since my cum had splashed his opening , he was presently right down to my balls. All my dick was absolutely inside him despite the fact that it was as of now not bloated.

He held my hands over his dick and started motioning the speed he preferred it. I didnt need to be narrow minded so I did as he needed me to. Few moments later, thick white sperm shot out of his dick and sprinkled all over. We held our situation for some time and afterward he got off me. We tidied up and dozed. All during that time I was unable to rest. My dick was rock hard and prepared for all the more however chuzie was at that point sleeping soundly.

****

Chuzie currently was a developed man. Smelt wonderful and appeared to be getting along admirably. Last time I knew about his whereabouts, I learned he was in Europe. He currently had bunches of tattoos and in his eyes, I could see he's had to deal with a hard parcel.

He proposed to take me out for a beverage and I let him know I expected to shower. Out of civility I welcomed him into my room I once imparted to my senior sibling who was adequately benevolent to leave practically the entirety of his hardware and device for my utilization after he moved out.

We left our mom's in the lounge room as they gosspied noisily.

I quickly expressed the reality to chuzie that I was unable to manage the cost of any of the things he found in the bed room in the event that he began having thoughts. While I arranged to shower, we started discussing activity and which piece of working out was generally troublesome. At that point, I was at that point on my towel and I could see his eyes fixed on my groin.

Chuzie looked exceptionally straight.

I excused each considered him being gay since certain individuals out develop something's they did as youthful grown-ups . He let me know he preferred naija jamz and requested that I play some for him. I associated my bluetooth speaker with my telephone and the Yemi Alade started sticking.

Myself and chuzie started thinking back about bygone eras and companions we've lost contact with.

Chuzie asked me for my telephone so he could go through my music records. I honestly gave him the telephone and as I was tied in with venturing into the restroom, he shouted ...

"EEEHHHHHH WHAT IS THIS????"

as I pivoted, I nearly blacked out from what I saw. He had tracked down his direction to my photograph exhibition and was checking out at my completely erect dick photograph. He waved my telephone at me as though to say "I have the proof".

I raced to recover my telephone from him however he was quicker than me. We both got into a genuine battle however as expected he over fueled me.

He had gotten on Top of me and prevailed with regards to holding my two gives over and utilizing his feet to lock mine. My towel has totally gone off my midriff and I was right there; lying bare under him.

Very much like bygone eras.

He investigated my eyes and his face was so near mine. I could smell his scent, the mint on his breath And anything that item he utilized on his facial hair.

He squeezed his crotch on mine and that gave me a moment hard on. I could feel his solid dick on me.

He carried his mouth nearer to mine however I moved my face away...i made sense of for him that I don't kiss somebody on the off chance that I am not in that frame of mind with the individual . At any rate, he recently snickered and did it. He kissed me so sluggishly that I in the long run gave hotel. He started licking my sweat-soaked body and tounging my soggy armpit. He went down to my dick and took me in his warm mouth.

It had been more than 7 months after my separation which additionally was the last time I engaged in sexual relations. What's more, since I am not a fan for wanking, having a mouth on my dick was electrifyingly marvelous.

While he profound throated me, he fixed his shorts.

I connected for my body cream and a sachet of condom at the top of my bed and gave it to him. As a rule, if he somehow happened to be my accomplice, I would have eaten his opening sore until it was sufficiently free to deal with my strike (bug spray can) comparable chicken and would have certainly gone sans protection . Yet, that was a lot of a distinction to be hard about so I kept myself.

Chuzie crushed a small bunch of cream and started dealing with my dick after he had slid down the condom (which sadly couldn't arrive at the foundation of my pole). His eyes gleamed with seething marvel. He got on top of me and stared at me. He looked like a legitimate "hard man" with the manner in which he grimaced with serious assurance as he took me.

This time he went right down . He rode me like a genuine steed. Pressing his butt hole muscles at whatever point he slid up my shaft. I went for his tore chest and got strong muscles. He realized I cherished his strong mass. He started flexing his mass like an Olympian as he did the front twofold bicep present. I was in a real sense falling head over heels for the load on top of me. I spat on my hand and went for his dick. It was as yet unchanged size and feel. Nothing has changed.

He went after my salve and spread it on himself in a sluggish erotic way. His elusive abs and chest sparkled like dark gold as he flexed them.

I was unable to help myself as I sat up and returned his push. We secured in sweet hug, kissing, perspiring... My hand stroking his soggy rooster , his butt-centric muscles kneading my curiously large dick skillfully, my slender muscle chest on his enormous cumbersome chest. This was out and out a one man to another activity.

Indeed, even with the discernible voices of our mom's coming from the living room, we had no expectations to be mindul or dial back. I beseeched him to screw my dick and he did precisely as I directed. "let me know when you need to cum" he groaned into our kiss and I gestured.

No sooner he murmured to me, did I murmur the appearance of my cream. With a strong push that nearly broken my balls, Chuzie held a long delay as he emphatically crushed his butt-centric wall muscles so hard that I felt my dick would snap down the middle. I could feel a tremendous help as though my body had delivered a long worrying about concern as my sperm overflowed the condom. Chuzie was at that point there too...soiling my hands and our gathering stomach with his man juice. We both kissed long and slow before he let me go.

Without beating around the bush, that was whenever I first had experience such staggering sex.

As I dropped back on the bed gasping for air, I felt him eliminate the condom from my dick. I peered down and could see that the condom was appropriately full. My entire stomach was brimming with cum as well as chuzie's. He as well; should have off stacked a ton.

He tracked down my receptacle and destroyed the condom. My head was pulsating somewhat and as I tried to sit up, I felt his mouth on my now practically limp dick once more. I helped him to remember our mom's nearby and he chuckled. We kissed momentarily and came to the restroom together to shower.

He let me know how he had been in jail in Europe and how he had endure difficulty. I inquired as to whether he did prostitution since deciding from his sex abilities, he could be mistaken for a top notch pornography star. He admitted he was seeing a white man who was base since he wanted papers . As per him, he possibly bottoms in the event that the dick is additional enormous and on the off chance that he "cherishes" the proprietor.

As he continued to commend my sex ability, all I did was giggle cos he really doesn't know around 50% of the oddity I am when am into somebody.

We advanced back to the parlor and later went out visiting spots of our young life.

Most likely I find chuzie truly and intellectually alluring. He's asked me out and I have acknowledged on the grounds we take as much time as is needed. I will update you as often as possible on how it turns out when I release my maximum capacity on him.

CHAPTER 2

My Enugu experience

I was educated in Enugu and lived piece of my life there also. I was constantly alluded to as nwa mummy or ajebo in light of my delicate nature which now and again became feminine when I was right at home. My temperament was the explanation my dad demanded I go to a firm stance all-male instructive foundation that would harden me up and make me shed my non-abrasiveness, since my mom had comprehensively wouldn't let him sending my sibling and I to a tactical school.

Ultimately my dad had his direction and I was trucked away from the solace of my home and non-public school toward the East to school. It was a bad dream, adapting in the Igbo-talking, unpleasant, all-young men school I was signed up for. in any case, I oversaw and passed from one class to another, and made a couple of companions en route.

And afterward I was in my senior class. Back then, in Enugu, there existed a problem area, a pool in a spot called the Sports Club. It was constantly topped off on ends of the week and was the most blazing spot around.

On this pivotal day, I visited the pool with my gay companions and they were completely banded together up, aside from me. The pool was bizarrely uncrowded for an end of the week, so there was less enjoyable to have. As we ate suya and jabbered, we as a whole seen the unexpected presence of a tall, darker looking, very much fabricated and bare headed person. His white shirt was an ideal differentiation to his brown complexion, and the blue denim pant was a decent match. He had a long goatee and the loot in his walk gave him gobs of character. He was a hot man, and we as a whole let it be known as we gazed.

At the point when this person went into the changing room and came out minutes after the fact, I was exceptionally satisfied with his constitution. It was obvious that he really buckled down since he had distinct muscles. In any case, his nylon loose shorts provided no insight with regards to what he was pressing. Right now, I was playing innocuously with one of my companions' accomplice, and we as a whole were enjoying a hearty chuckle.

How about you find yourself a man, my companion's accomplice out of nowhere inquired.

It's difficult, I answered.

No be man wey full here, another companion expressed, motioning at the pool, inside which were just guys.

See that fine person that strolled in, my companion's accomplice prodded. How about you go for himself and let us be?

Right away, my blood bubbled. Is that a challenge, I said.

Indeed, I twofold challenge you, he tested cheerfully.

What's more, I got up from my seat, adapting to the situation.

I strolled to the pool's edge and took a jump. There was some water sprinkling meeting happening between two groups and Mister Tall-Dark-And-Handsome was important for the game. I joined his group of splashers, and on second thought of me sprinkling our rivals, I angrily sprinkled him. There was a lot of chuckling at this, and much water all over the place. Before long, in any case, the meeting was finished.

This person, you be saboteur o, he prodded as he swam dependent upon me.

Pardon me jaré, I laughed while loosening up my hand. I presented myself.

He grasped my hand in a firm shake and presented himself as Osas. See as your hand delicate, once more, he prodded, snickering.

Before long, we were talking away like lifelong companions, and I got to realize he visited Enugu periodically to manage his dad's organization; this was one of such visits. He was from Benin and lived in Lagos. He was an extremely insightful man and talked persuasively. We discussed the economy, sports, states in Nigeria that shook, music. Lastly, he said in a purposeful Benin emphasize, Omoh, wey darlings nah! I gossip angels dey come here well.

Immediately, my disposition changed. He continued to continue endlessly about how he was hoping to meet young ladies, blah, blah, blah. I hesitantly let him know I was additionally very amazed at the all male presence at the pool. There was no single female around, indeed, aside from an exceptionally chunky lady who accompanied her children and was showing them how to swim under the oversight of a similarly husky man who no question was her significant other.

Obviously, Osas was disturbed. He continued onward on about ladies, and when he saw I held no interest for the subject, he playfully said, You sef, this one you keep calm like say you no like lady. Abi you be brought back to life or fag? Which one you be? As he talked, he sprinkled some water in front of me (I surmise he did that so I could comprehend he was kidding).

Brought back to life ke! I look like minister? I inquired.

Yet, why your body simply change when you hear lady? Abi you no get geh companion? he inquired.

Indeed I no get. Abi you wan scramble me your sister? I terminated back.

Wetin dey dia? I for run you my sister nah! Yet, as she wear wed wetin you need make I do?

You and this your lady talk, e be like you be ashawo, I said.

Giggling, he answered, No ooo! I barely get time due to work, however whenever I find the opportunity, I dey get my pleasant o! In any case, I love pussy, mehn.

I shrugged my shoulders and shook my head. I was plainly bothered.

That's what he saw, and he said, This person, wetin you be sef? You be reverend dad? Why you dey do this way? I dey suspect you o! E be like you be fag.

Indeed, I be fag. Thus? Na new tin? Goody gumdrops, free me abeg, I spat out strongly.

Chei! He hollered and began snickering once more. He probably thought I was joking.

I didn't go along with him in that frame of mind; rather I gazed vacantly at him.

Mehn, bobo, without a doubt. You're joking, correct? he asked as his chuckling subsided.

A curve of my temple was all the reaction I gave him. Furthermore, he became gazed at me, obviously dumbfounded. We had been visiting like mates for quite a while, and had constructed a compatibility, felt truly OK with one another. So the striking step I took with conceding my sexuality to him was something I thought he wouldn't take outrageous. I calculated that the most terrible thing that could happen would be him letting me know he didn't connect with my sort, and that would be it. Other than he came alone, didn't live in Enugu and two of the folks that were collaborated with my companions were military officials, so I realized I was protected from any A.

For what reason should a fine person as you do such? He asked then. Might it be said that you fear ladies? Any lady would pass on to have you. Do you realize God is against this?

So God isn't against you coming to the pool to search for pussies, I promptly cut in.

He was quiet again for certain seconds, and afterward he said, But could you wed and have children?

Must I be a spouse to be a dad, I immediately replied.

Once more he hushed up.

Osas, I have been this way for my entire life, I expressed discreetly to him. Since youth, it's anything but a decision. I love men. I love dicks, brother. I have had my toll portion of pussy I actually favor cocks. Not my shortcoming.

He was dumbstruck by my strength. Kai, I don't really accept that this, he at long last mumbled. Do your folks be aware? How would you appreciate sex with another man? What's the pleasantness in ridiculously a poop hole? How man go dey humble me? This last part he seemed to tell himself as he shook his head vivaciously, as though shaking off a few prohibited considerations.

Perhaps a few of us like to be lowered, I said.

How? Kindly make sense of, he said, evidently inquisitive.

Then, at that point, my long talk on tops and versatiles and bottoms and the ABC of gay sex began. He focused, with a slight grimace

So which one do you do? He at long last inquired.

I'm adaptable, I answered, yet I'm more gifted in getting.

As in, you appreciate getting screwed more? He inquired.

Indeed, I said.

If it's not too much trouble, stop this, I'm imploring you. You are my sibling, mehn. It's a wrongdoing.

Says who? I harnessed. I began citing sacred texts that likewise censured blending textures, eating from a tree, shaving and gathering interests from credits. I discussed how man would effectively obliterate each other, regardless of whether it implied choosing a section from any sacred book to legitimize his mischievousness. Indeed, even Jesus Christ was killed on grounds of conflicting with the sacred writings.

He was amazed at my profundity of information on religion, yet he said tenaciously, You really want to stop this, brother. I'm certain you haven't seen a dick that will make you lament this demonstration.

At this, I giggled. And afterward, I laughed at him, discussing how I was a gifted power base and how unimaginable it was that any dick would make me lament being gay. As I would like to think, no such dick existed.

He took a gander at me for some time and said I ought to be figured an example, one which would eliminate the franticness from my head. Sooner or later, he said he expected to return to his lodging, and I inquired as to whether I could go along. Show up then, at that point, assuming you have the guts you say you have, he said.

I unexpectedly felt a surge of fervor. It appeared to be this would have been another sexual experience, one I was certain I planned to appreciate completely. I went to say my farewells to my companions, who were staggered when I gladly educated them that I was leaving with Mister Tall-Dark-And-Handsome. A few minutes after the fact, Osas left the evolving room, spruced up. He got together where I was with my companions, and there were handshakes and good tidings. I expressed farewell to my companions and left with Osas, not understanding what I was finding myself mixed up with.

We took a ride to the Guest Inn, where he was remaining. We got into his room and he requested a few beverages for us. Sometimes he would see me, laugh briskly and shake his head. He pardoned himself and went into the restroom. By then, I attempted to be exceptionally perceptive of the environmental factors, in the event that he was into some cash custom business. Nonetheless, when I saw the records and a few reports on the bed and table which had his dad's organization name on them, I was more loose. I went to the restroom entryway and tuned in, attempting to hear what was happening on the opposite side of the entryway. I heard the murmuring hints of inward breath; I could likewise see it. He was taking Indian hemp. I shook my head and laughed delicately as I strolled back to the bed. Removing my shoes and shirt, I set down on the bed and paused.

A couple of moments later, Osas ventured into the room. He looked stoned. His eyes were blushed and he looked quiet and ascertaining. He plunked down on a seat. He had changed his shorts and was topless like me. He was lovely. I veered over to where he sat and in the middle of between his thighs. They were enormous and strong. His eyes were shut and he had his face somewhat covered with his right hand.

Is it true that you are alright? I inquired. What is on your mind?

I'm fine, mehn, he replied. Furthermore, he opened his red eyes, grinned momentarily. He had on an odd articulation. The grin immediately evaporated; he muttered something to himself and shut his eyes, putting his hand over his face once more.

I began kissing his strong body and sucking on his areolas. He stood by. At the point when my hands began moving towards his crotch, he immediately held them and woke up.

I saw an alternate individual. A risky looking individual. Furthermore, interestingly, I was apprehensive. From the get go, I was anticipating a hard slap or something like that. Also, assuming this person ought to endeavor beating me, he would kill me.

You said you could stop homosexuality, correct? He inquired.

My heart was pulsating quick, and I was unable to express anything accordingly.

OK, he responded to his inquiry. Since you demanded following me, you should consent to take anything that it is I have. Bargain? His voice was cold.

Haven't we discussed this? I said, grinning shakingly, wanting to facilitate the strained environment.

Bargain? he rehashed.

OK fine. Bargain, I replied.

He set my hands free from his hold, and afterward I proceeded with the body love. At the point when my hand got to his dick, I froze. My palms felt something exceptionally wide. It wasn't bloated at this point. However, the width made my heart sink and got my circulatory strain dashing. Osas separated his legs to give my hands more space to meander over his groin.

Monstrous is putting it mildly. His dick was startling. He woke up and had on an extremely underhanded grin. You no dey dread, abi? He said smoothly. My companion, suck my dick.
I felt so cold. I naturally realized I needed to obey on the grounds that he was under impact and could be fit for outrageous viciousness assuming I denied. Stuffing his dick into my mouth was an issue. What's more, sucking it was a battle. The more I sucked him, the more his dick appeared to increment long and bigness.

Goody gumdrops, suck that prick! Suck am well, he directed.

I truly needed to get away, to be away from my ongoing situation. Perhaps on the off chance that I could make him cum with a sensual caress, maybe I could save my unfortunate ass from destruction. Preparing myself and taking a full breath, I applied each sensual caress expertise I knew, trusting I would get this nigga shooting some cum. I just prevailed with regards to making him stand most of the way from the seat so he could screw my mouth. I stifled as he called me names softly. Then he said, You go ability far today. He fixed and strolled to the TV. My goodness! He was a divine being. What's more, his dick resembled a god from a place of worship. He tracked down Channel O and expanded the volume.

Then he got back to me. Going after my pant, he yanked them off me. Pull it off speedy, he yelped as he stood, wanking his dick like to keep the erection.

I was thinking quick. I was fighting to keep my mental stability. If it's not too much trouble, cream… do you have cream, I said pleadingly. The last thing I needed was a tear and I was certain it was conceivable he might endeavor to enter me without grease.

He got a Pears child oil, poured an on all fours the container to me. As I spread a liberal sum on all fours my butt, I watched him rub the oil on his chicken and stomach, making it focus and glister on the bulb light. Quickly he held my foot and hauled me to the edge of the bed.

Oya, open am, he yapped. I said open it!

I raised my legs high, and as I watched him twist with his dick in his grasp, I started begging him, Please relax… Osas please…

As I felt his dick on my butt-centric entry, I heard him murmur, Your fada! Furthermore, he went in.

White light blazed in my mind as his dick got itself into my butt. I let out a quiet shout as my eyes broadened. I could feel Osas in my stomach in a real sense. He was areas of strength for excessively drive away. He held my lower legs and squeezed them to the bed. Each foot near my ear. He screwed me like a frantic bull and continued to murmur, I will show you today. I dug my nails into his chest and began hitting him. We got into a little battle and afterward he grasped my neck tight. Try not to fuck with me, he murmured. With bizarre readiness, he turned me like a cloth doll on my stomach. His solid shaggy legs nailed down mine and one of his enormous hands held both of mine which was currently at my back. Unexpectedly, there was a hot blaze in my mind. He had entered my butt once more. It seemed like he just infiltrated me interestingly. His other free hand snatched my shoulder to direct my body to meet his pushing.

I will screw you like a bitch! He gasped. Come on, open your nyash!

Tears gushed from my eyes. It seemed like until the end of time. Please accept my apologies, kindly stop, I whimpered in anguish. I battled under him and it seemed like the more I did, the more my butt-centric muscles crushed on his dick, giving him more delight. He tossed his weight on me, lay on my back. He was extremely weighty. I felt his hands part my butt cheeks as he continued to hammer profound into me.

You need dick ba? You need dick, abi? He continued to gasp into my ear.

Noooo, noooo please noooo, I cried.

You never begin to cry, he crowed. What's more, he expanded his beat.

I chose to unwind and profess to appreciate it, since it appeared to be the more I battled and asked, the more he determined his pleasure. Screw me daddy! I started to groan. Gracious screw me! Give me that dick.

I'm simply beginning, he answered. I will give you.

He moved to his back while as yet having me in his grasp. This time, he held my hands from under my armpit to my neck. My penis was up high and I was confronting the roof. His beast dick was still a lot of covered somewhere inside me and siphoning fiercely. I took a gander at the time; I could barely handle it. It was an hour and 45 minutes previously gone in horrifying torment.

All of a sudden, there was a thump on the entryway and we both froze. He delivered his grasp and I escaped into the latrine. I could hear voices through the entryway. It appeared somebody thumped on some unacceptable entryway, since I heard conciliatory sentiments. I needed to sit on the latrine seat in light of the fact that my legs were shaking. My butt hole expanded and it was a marvel I wasn't dying. I began crying.

There was a delicate thump on the entryway and Osas called out to me. I didn't reply. Once more, he called and said I ought to kindly open the entryway. I did and returned to the latrine to plunk down. He came in after me; he had his fighters on, yet his dick was still unshakable. He laughed and crouched before me.

Did I hurt you, he asked delicately.

I didn't reply. I was unable to try and see his face.

Are you harmed, once more, he asked.

I shook my head and said no.

See, you caused this, he said. You caused me to do this. Yet, I believe that you should know I'm not the kind of individual to hurt another person. Check out at me now. He turned my face to meet his. He looked so quiet and sweet. Nothing at all like the beast who had assaulted me minutes sooner.

Please accept my apologies, alright? He said.

I didn't answer.

Standing up, he pulled me dependent upon him and embraced me. Dislike this, truly, he said. I believe you should get to know me seriously. Grin now, Haba! Yet, you were the one making all the commotion naw. He was attempting his damnedest to support me.

And afterward, shockingly, he kissed my brow, took my face in his grasp and kissed me completely all the rage. His kiss was so warm and delicate. And afterward, he drove me back to the room. He started enlightening me concerning how ladies take off from his dick, about how he needed to turn to putting off the light before sex so they wouldn't get to see what he planned to screw them with.

He proceeded to say that he truly delighted in sex with me and that for sure I was areas of strength for a.

I need to see you once more, he said. We should begin a new page. Allow me to make this dependent upon you.

I sat discreetly in my corner, with my butt breathing fire.

He drew nearer to me and kissed me again all the rage, squeezed and fidgeted with my areolas, kissed my neck, chest and sucked on my areolas. This beast was making delicate love to me and I despised my body for answering his touch. He squeezed me back on the bed and touched my exposed body.

Gee, so this is the very thing that gays appreciate, eh? He said happily. So you have prevailed with regards to making me gay with your sweet ass. He giggled this time.

He was so attractive and lovely, yet something inside me passed on and left me unfeeling.

I'm still hard… I need to cum, he mumbled.

Hearing that gave me a shock. You are not putting that thing inside me, Osas, I protested.

If it's not too much trouble, if it's not too much trouble, let me just cum, he persuaded. My dick won't go down. I guarantee I won't put everything inside. I will be delicate. If it's not too much trouble, believe me.

He continued his stroking and profound kissing as he laid back on top of me. He spat on all fours my butt. Gradually he entered me, yet as he guaranteed, he didn't place the whole length in. He was delicate and his pushes had a kind of mood. He kissed me all through the ride and afterward he started to snort and inhale intensely. His body began to shudder as he groaned, Oh no, goodness, no.

I felt hot rolls of cum shoot somewhere inside my butt again and again. My entrail was brimming with his seed. He imploded alongside me and held me.

Amazing, this is great, he panted. Don't you need to cum?

No, I'm fine.

I can screw you the entire day, you know, he radiated. You have a smooth and delicate ass and body.

I felt unpleasant bile ascend in my throat at his words. My mum is visiting the area and I really want to return home, I lied then, at that point.

If it's not too much trouble, guarantee you will return before I go, he said, like he could have read my mind.

I don't have any idea yet I will attempt, I lied once more.

I got up and spruced up, and at the entryway, he embraced me.

Allow me to cherish you, he said. Allow me that opportunity.

I basically gestured. As he strolled me outside to where I would get a taxi, he drew out a heap of naira notes and said it was his olive branch. I said nothing him as he stuck the roll into my pant pocket. What's more, soon, I was returning. Away from him.

I never called him. I didn't return to see him. For a considerable length of time, I had no sexual longing. Indeed, even masturbation aggravated me. Osas wrecked my psyche. I don't have the foggiest idea where he is or what has befallen him and his beast dick, however I will always remember that sex story that started at the pool.

CHAPTER 3

AKPAN AND I

During my senior optional school days, I generally joined my property manager's children to school in their vehicle since they went through the course to my school, and that was an extraordinary comfort. It was likewise a slight burden in light of the fact that since they generally got up right off the bat to beat the typical morning gridlock in the city of Port Harcourt, I needed to get up early as well.

On this portentous morning, I got up curiously early. I was spruced up for school and was sitting ceaselessly. I realized my landowner's youngsters wouldn't be prepared at that point; I anyway chose to go hang tight for them outside their cabin until they were prepared to leave.

It was around a couple of moments past 5am when I got into their compound. The compound was dead peaceful and void, aside from Akpan, one of their drivers, who was washing the vehicle. I'd seen Akpan consistently and never checked out him.

Until that morning.

He ordinarily wore a free-streaming tunic during the daytime, and one could figure he was a wide man from his level and the region of his shoulders. Akpan seemed to be in his 40s, an extremely calm and respectful man. He was normal with regards to looks, yet his stocky form, brown complexion and full facial hair made him seem to be a man of character.

Toward the beginning of that day, when I saw him, I created chills. Also, that didn't have anything to do with the cold of the early morning. He was clad just in white fighters, one that was freely fitting and wet from his washing of the vehicle. Thusly, the whole state of his mammoth chicken was noticeable. His legs seemed to be the bark of an oak tree in a tropical jungle. Thick, solid and covered with hairs. His chest was wide and formed. Dull and lavishly sprinkled with hair.

How in paradise did I have such a divine being near and didn't see him? I asked myself. I was unable to take my eyes off the striking engraving of his chicken against his fighters. Indeed, even with the morning chill and the virus sprinkle of water, his dick didn't look contracted.

I strolled nearer to him, welcomed him and inquired as to whether I could assist him with topping off the can he was utilizing to wash the vehicle. He grinned and said I shouldn't annoy, that I could soil my uniform. I said it wouldn't make any difference and I took the pail and strolled to the tap. I could hear his voice after me, saying, 'God favor you, sir.' I grinned to myself and thought, Indeed, He favored me when He let me see you in this express earlier today.

Over the course of that day in class, I was unable to think. I needed to go to the school latrine to jack off to have the option to appropriately think. Not entirely settled to fashion an associate with

Akpan, and when I decided to do that, there was no halting me. I began attempting to invest energy with him, expanding little tokens of benevolence all the while. I purchased another arrangement of hued fighter shorts for himself and let him know I could have done without the one he wore that morning, since it was old. That was valid; I additionally could have done without it since I didn't need anybody seeing his bundle as far as I could tell that morning. Once in a while, I would give him a few cash, get him a few baked goods and little things of dress. Each time I offered him grace, he would agree 'Thank you' in the humblest voice I'd heard, constantly without visually connecting. I thought that he was either an alien to cherish and mind, or had been harmed previously.

We fostered a decent yet provisional companionship; it was cheerful, and he appeared to see the value in it almost however much I did.

During one of those times of fuel shortage and resulting climb of the value, he was told by his chief, my landowner, to proceed to line up for fuel. It was an errand most street clients knew about. Holding up vast hours in line to be sold fuel. On this specific night, my mom had voyaged and I was home alone, so I chose to go for a walk. That was the point at which I saw him drive towards me. I asked him where he was going, and he let me know he planned to line for fuel for the evening. This was around 8pm, and I realized he could wind up returning the following day in the event that he was fortunate to be sold fuel. Feeling my heart start a little palpitation, I inquired as to whether I could go along with him. He assented. I got into the vehicle and we drove off to the filling station.
True to form, the line was interminable. We drove behind one vehicle and he killed the motor. We started talking and sharing individual encounters. He informed me concerning his better half leaving him, and taking their two youngsters with her, due to his penury and powerlessness to take legitimate consideration of them. His significant other was remarried. What's more, his trust for womenfolk was harmed.

All through our discussion, I struggled a hard-on. The day was far spent. The weather conditions was cool, and a shower had begun outside. I leaned back on my seat, and he did likewise, removing his shirt simultaneously. We kept talking, however I essentially couldn't take my eyes off his bushy chest. The chest hair looked wonderful and grass like, not elastic and harsh. I commended him and inquired as to whether I could contact the hair. He laughed and expressed something about me taking care of business like him, and how it was anything but no joking matter. I began contacting his chest, feather-like contacts that I realized he delighted in on the grounds that he let me know it was a sweet touch he could be enticed to work off.

Since it was dim, I wasn't extremely certain on the off chance that my eyes saw a lump in his groin, or whether it was my creative mind. I needed to be aware without a doubt. So I inquired as to whether he was wearing one of the fighters I got him. He said OK. I inquired as to whether he really discarded the old white one I saw him in a few days ago. He said he did that quite a while. With a funny tone, I inquired as to whether I could see which one he was by and by wearing. He pulled at the highest point of the clothing over his pants to show me. I connected my hand to contact the texture, and simultaneously, I nonchalantly broadened my last finger toward his groin to affirm assuming he had an erection. He did indeed! My finger contacted what felt like steel. My mouth went dry and my heart started to pulsate quicker. In any case, I didn't dare to begin petting the erection; I would have rather not taken a chance with culpable him. Be that as it may, I kept my hand on the fighter while I discussed picking the texture and the fighters. Precum was at that point overflowing from my enlarged dick. Unexpectedly he said he needed to ease himself, and requested that I stay in the vehicle to avoid lowlifes. I wanted to follow him to see his enlarged dick while he peed.

At the point when Akpan at long last returned, I saw the lump was no more. I felt a slight pull of disillusionment. He didn't plunk down inside the vehicle for some time; rather he strolled forward, searching for how to get fuel. A couple of hours passed before we needed to purchase from the bootleg market. And afterward, we were returning.

It wasn't some time before individuals around started to see my closeness with Akpan, particularly his companion bunch, which comprised of the entryway man of my compound and that of the landowner, as well as his three different drivers. Now and again, when they saw me coming, they'd call out to out him and say his "smallie" was near. This quipping normally made me timid.
And afterward came the end of the week when my mom headed out to the town to see her mom. Once more, I was home alone. I had quite recently completed my clothing and was hanging my garments out to dry in the patio, when I heard Akpan's voice lifted in clearly giggling with the gateman of my compound. I heard him inquire as to whether I was home, and I felt a surge of serious delight. I had tied one of my long sleeved shirts round my midriff and was bare under, seeing as there was nobody home and I was perspiring unnecessarily from the clothing. I shouted to him from the terrace since I was unable to emerge to the front with only a shirt around my midriff, and furthermore in light of the fact that I didn't believe he should try thumping at the front entryway. He came around the house with an immense grin all over. The surge of delight I felt escalated such a lot of I needed to battle to pack it down. I lifted my right hand high in a hand shake signal, and he slapped it tenderly away, maneuvering me into a fast embrace all things considered. His chest was strong as block and his hold was savage. What's more, I heard the thunder of my pulse at such nearness sound in my ears. Good gracious, what a man…

We talked a little, with him enquiring about my mom's whereabouts and me getting some information about the outing he took with his oga, the property manager. He'd taken the man and his family away, and return to Port Harcourt without them. He referenced he was on a task to the specialist, and would attempt to return around when he was finished. As he left, my heart started to race. I was so energized. My mum wasn't home, similar to his chief. We both had our available energy and I needed to utilize it.

I held up external the door of my compound for seemingly endlessness. I needed to see Akpan return; I was unable to sit tight for him to determine the status of me. At the point when it started pouring and the lights went out, I needed to return inside the house. Because of the weariness from my washing, I napped off. When I awakened, it was exceptionally late, a couple of moments to 10pm. Goodness! How might I get hold of Akpan? I immediately spruced up and set out toward the door. As I drew nearer, I could hear a gathering of men snickering. Clearly it was Akpan's club, doing some male tattle. I truly supplicated Akpan would be outside with them as I moved toward the entryway. He was. He was the principal individual I saw when I got to the men. At the point when he saw me, he called out to out me, and asked facetiously in the event that I'd been with a lady inside this time the power had been off. Everybody giggled. My gateman answered that no female had at any point come to search for me, that I was a decent kid. Akpan said it was an insightful man who might stay away from ladies since they were perilous. Also, very much like that, the discussion fixated on ladies and every one of the manners in which they had harmed humanity. The men started offering their sexual capers to the various ladies in their lives. It was the sort of talk that exhausted me, and I needed to return in. I anyway couldn't on the grounds that my Akpan was still outside. At around 11pm, they all started to scatter, leaving just me, Akpan and my landowner's gateman on the wooden seat.

At the point when Akpan asked the gateman assuming they siphoned water into the tank - in light of the fact that he needed to wash - the gateman answered that the property manager's better half locked the siphoning machine and left with the key. That implied there would be no water in the tank until the family returned. What he, the gateman, had saved for himself was as a matter of fact water from the downpour that fell. The two men protested about the clear underhandedness of their courtesan for a couple of seconds, before the gateman chose to resign. Akpan was apparently hopeless. He grumbled a few additional about the ills of being the assistance, particularly to the landowner. He discussed how he needed to share the little space of the young men's quarters with the other three men that were in the property manager's utilize. I was alarmed. I knew exactly how little the young men's quarters convenience was. Also, with four men consuming the room, the day to day environment would be awful. I felt sympathy for him as he kept whining about his general situation. I opened my passed available to him and checked him out. He took a gander at my hand and took it in his. 'You will be fine sometime in the future, trust God,' I said consolingly. 'So be it,' he answered.

It was truly late then, at that point. I advised him to accompany me. He denied. I persuaded him, promising him a decent shower and a nice feast. He thought for some time and yielded, saving a couple of moments to go illuminate the gateman of his compound to secure, before he returned and strolled with me into my home.

Inside the house, Akpan sat on the couch and I went to put on the generator and microwaved a plate of jollof rice and goat meat for him. Furthermore, when the dinner was finished, I brought it out to the lounge area, alongside a glass of cold water and a jug of chilled brew. I was excited to serve him, felt a decent, loyal housewife, taking special care of the necessities of her man of some sort or another.

I called him to the lounge area. He appeared to be enjoyably amazed by what I spread out for him. At the point when he got some information about my own food and I let him know I was fine, he requested I bring an additional spoon and go along with him. I flippantly said I had placed an adoration mixture into the food so he that he would cherish me. He chuckled at that, saying that it would be an exercise in futility, and assuming I was a lady, he could never have disapproved. Goodness, yet not set in stone to change all that. We ate together, bantering as we ate and perspiring from the moistness. I could see he wanted a shower, so after I tidied up out the table, I went to run the water for his shower.
I completed my end of the year tests and my outcomes was fabulous. Gbemiga was ecstatic on the grounds that he had forever been empowering, coaching and persuading me to be awesome. He was the dad and sibling I won't ever have.

At the point when aunt Pamela got back from any place she went to, Gbemiga told her of my outcomes and all she could say was ..."so?...after all... different children are improving. "

"what kind of proclamation is that lady? What in the world do you mean?"

Gbemiga asked with aggravation.

"meaning he won't become anything throughout everyday life. He will be basically as pointless as his father....or would it be advisable for me I say mother. Between the two Of them sef I don't have the foggiest idea who is driving" she said while chuckling at her joke.

I didn't have the foggiest idea when tears started tumbling from my eyes. Presently; I have seen Gbemiga furious however never have I seen him free his cool the manner in which he did when he checked me out. Indeed, even aunt Pamela was shocked. He addressed aunt Pamela in a way that it required her minutes to answer. He called her a callous Harlot and reviled the day he met her. She was tied in with offering her expression of "I gave you life" and before the words left her mouth, Gbemiga terminated at her. He told her he worked for his cash and was no spouse of hers. "really!!!!!! so the thing are you doing under my rooftop?" aunt Pamela seethed in protection as she was red and working out of fiendish annoyance.

"I will move out of your rooftop and go to the young men quarter assuming that will make you regard yourself . The arrangement we had on my agreement expressed that a convenience was the reward".

He started pressing his things. Aunt Pamela started applauding over his head and continued to rain affronts. Letting him know a lady is taking care of him and he was no man.

Seeing all the show was humiliating to the point that I wanted to be in the house. The two of them truly uncovered themselves and I heard alot.

At the point when it was prepared, I called him to the restroom. He was satisfied by my persevering through token of consideration, and said as much. This time, he added that he wished I was a lady.

Why, I said.

Since you know how to show great cherishing, he answered.

Does it truly matter on the off chance that I'm not a lady, I inquired. Furthermore, how might a lady at any point respond that a man can't do other than conceiving an offspring, I needed to be aware.

A lady has an opening, he said with a laugh.

Automatically, I answered, 'Thus do I.'

At that, he went to gaze curiously at me. What do you mean, he inquired. Why? Where could the opening be?

For reasons unknown, the inquiries and his questionable articulation caused me to feel both hurt and inconvenience. What's more, they displayed all over. I got up from the seat to leave. He hurriedly held my hand. He asked me where I was going to. I answered tersely, advised him to proceed to meet a lady with an opening. He grinned liberally at me and told me not to be irate. I sulked a little, and asked him again to go have his shower. Sure that he had insulted me, he was sorry. Reluctant to destroy the evening, I acknowledged the statement of regret and added brazenly that I couldn't want anything more than to go along with him in the washroom.

Or on the other hand would you like a lady all things considered, I added.

I maintain that my lady should go along with me, he answered with a sharp look at me and a laugh.

That satisfied me definitely.

In the restroom, it wasn't some time before he shed his garments. Seeing him obvious exposed was a thing of beauty. It evaporated my mouth and made me battle for breath. I attempted to will down the erection I could feel coming. Gracious God… !

We got into the bath, and he before long started wiping himself. Energetically. I advised him to dial back. I took the wipe from him and began washing his body, feeling my body shake with each contact my lathery hands made with his body.

What's up with you, he abruptly inquired.

What do you mean, I answered.

Wetin be this, he expressed, peering down. I followed his gaze to my dick, feeling no modest quantity of embarrassment when I saw that I was completely erect.

He jabbed at my erection with a finger, and inquired as to why I was turned on.

Perhaps this is on the grounds that I love you, I said, pausing my breathing.

There was an uncomfortable silence. He didn't express anything accordingly. I was sorry and begun washing myself. He requested to wash me as I'd done him. So I passed the wipe to him and turned my back to him. I felt him pour water on me. I felt the wipe on me. I felt his fingers dive into my skin. He commended my skin, said it was wonderful. I said thanks to him, however I didn't hear him. I was shudder, faint with want. My dick was stressing forward, pounding so hard I felt like I was going to cum any second.

Your body is moving me, I heard him out of nowhere mumble.

His voice was thick, the tone unsure and interesting simultaneously. What's more, it incited me to pivot to confront him.

Ruler Almighty!

He was hard. Rock hard! That dick of his that I'd continuously fantasized about was enlarged and extending out at me. It was asking to be contacted. I checked him out. He laughed reluctantly. That was all the support I wanted. I contacted him. I held his dick. I held his dick with my fingers, and they couldn't get altogether around the shaft. He was simply gigantic.

He gave another unsure laugh, and said he realized it was too enormous, and that his ex had detested engaging in sexual relations with him. He added that no man had an opening to oblige his dick.

What is he - a student?

I immediately stooped before him, and gazed intently, respectfully at that dick. It was so gorgeous but then it was appalling. There was an organization of veins all around its length. With each touch from my fingers, it pulsated and jolted fitfully. My mouth watered. I set my lips against the tip and kissed it. He let me know in an imposing voice to stop. In any case, we both knew better. There was no halting me, no halting us now.

I affectionately kissed the handle once more, prior to taking the thick shaft, many inchs, down my throat. He breathed out. I arrived at my hands up to his furry chest, and ran my hands all around the strong wall. And afterward down to his crotches. His balls were enormous and a small bunch. I sucked on them gradually. I stroked his dick which was clammy with my spit and his precum. I stood up and held him close. He held me as well, and our lips met. The kiss was profound and enthusiastic, and loaded up with guarantees. He kissed me, not due to the joy he got from it, but since he felt something. I sucked his areolas, armpits, each and every spot my tongue and mouth could track down on his body. His body shuddered as I attacked his body with my kisses. Eventually, I contemplated whether he was crying, since I heard a periodic quieted sniffs coming from him. Or on the other hand maybe he was sniffing away the wetness from our shower getting into his nose. I couldn't have cared less. I needed him. Terrible!
He held me and he kissed me as well. His hands were all around my body, generally getting at my skin as though to tear my body separated. His hands ran down my plumber's butt delicately and naturally I pivoted. He started crushing my chest as though I had bosoms. Our bodies were as yet wet and dangerous, as was my plumber's butt. I went after his dick and scoured it against my plumber's butt. He groaned. I groaned. He probably had a ton of precum, in light of the fact that the handle of his dick was exorbitantly soggy. I got a brief look at our appearance in the restroom reflect all of a sudden, and it was something else. A thinly fabricated, fair looking person squeezed facing a capably constructed, darker looking man. It was a sight I invited.

It felt right.

Also, no surprises there. At the point when he asked me, in a reluctant voice, on the off chance that I was certain this was correct, assuming I needed it, I gestured, and said OK.

Simply go gradually, child, please, gradually, I told him.

Akpan reclined and opened my butt cheeks with his two hands so his dick was very much focused on the objective that was my poop hole. Brilliant sparkles shot through my head and streams of sweet torment flooded inside me as he started heading inside. Cold surges dashed up my spine to my mind. His dick was heading inside. That magnificent beast was making its entry. I could feel my rectum separating. I started pressing and delivering my sphincter to loosen up the muscles. As my butt extended, I cycle my lower lip and took in a full breath. I needed to own this. I was unable to surrender now. That's what I thought assuming I did, Akpan could at absolutely no point ever endeavor it in the future. To make this work - to change over him - I would need to satisfy him quite well, and don't take anything back.

After seemingly forever, I at last felt his thick pubic hair on my butt, and his chest hair on my back. He was all inside.

Gracious child, I love you, he told me. You are mine, he proceeded. Could you at any point feel me inside?

I answered with a groan. I was completely involved. I felt like I'd gulped a truck. My stomach was full. Gradually he drove out and afterward back inside. Delicately and affectionately. He held me tight, ran his hands over me. And afterward he inquired as to whether he could cum. I turned my head to energetically meet his and kissed him. That was my response. He eliminated his lips from mine and reclined once more. He separated my butt cheeks to see his dick inside my butt. He started fucking me hard. On the mirror, I could see the glare of fixation all over. His huge hands went after my shoulders and he snorted, 'Take it currently, child.' And with a strong push that made them smother a shout of both desolation and delight, I felt his dick throb in my butt. He snorted and held me firmly, his body jolting as he shot his heap inside me. We stood like that briefly, until his body was still. And afterward he ground his dick more profound inside my butt, clearly cherishing the sensation of his cum inside my butt.

You are in excess of a lady, he mumbled with a laugh against my ear. Also, we both snickered delicately at that.

Subsequent to washing and drying our bodies, we went into my room. I could see he actually wasn't happy with what had simply occurred.

Will God be furious with us, he needed to be aware.

God needs to concede our heart wants, and I see nothing off-base on the off chance that our heart want is to be cherished and give love, I expressed reassuringly as I embraced him from behind. He held my hand as I added, Besides what we did was express what we feel for one another.

He gestured gradually, letting the heaviness of my words sink into his psyche. He was sorry for infiltrating me, and said he trusted he hadn't harmed me. I felt exceptionally sensitive down there, however it was basically impossible that I planned to let him know that. Rather I kissed him and inquired as to whether he truly appreciated been inside me. He conceded that it was a new and extremely sweet experience for him. He snatched my body and pulled me near him. Then he kissed me, and afterward went for my areolas and sucked on them. I groaned and jerked, in light of the fact that he continued to bite them.
Some way or another, through the cloudiness of my craving, I recalled that I needed to secure the entryways. I pardoned myself, however before I left the room, I put on the DVD player in my room and squeezed play. There was a macho fucker DVD inside the machine and I needed to make Akpan OK with what I trusted would have been his new sexuality. When I returned into the room, it was too meet a demeanor of paralyzed doubt all over. He clearly couldn't completely accept that such pornography

existed. He had loads of inquiries for me. Was this genuine? Was it film stunt? What pleasure did they get from it? Was it sweet? On the TV screen was a strong individual of color going at the ass of a white kid with his tongue and mouth; the kid was groaning into a cushion. That's what I cherished. What's more, I told Akpan.

Following a couple of moments, he switched off the TV and let me know I shouldn't ruin him. At the point when he said that he could have done without observing such, I thought it was on the grounds that it was gay pornography. However at that point he said that he felt sex ought to be regarded, and not be videoed. He could have done without straight pornography by the same token. I figured out his opinions.

From that point, I switched off the generator and opened the windows. I got into bed with him, and the whole room was overflowed with the silver light of the moon. I was content. I was as yet horny as well. So I kissed him once more, stroking him as I did. I went down to his groin; he was hard once more, and the dick possessed a scent like cleanser. I licked it. Furthermore, I gulped it. Furthermore, I sucked it. He started breathing vigorously as I sucked his balls. My tongue followed the path that rushed to his butt hole and afterward I tracked down the spot. It was so little. I started to tongue his poop hole as I affectionately wanked his dick. He curved his back and opened his legs more extensive. His butt was bushy and I showered it with fondness from my mouth.

After certain minutes, he pulled me up and held me to his chest. The number of individuals that have you done this with, he needed to be aware.

Does it matter, I answered.

He let go of me and sat up on the bed.

For what reason are you misbehaving, I said exasperatedly. Did I ask you what number of ladies you have engaged in sexual relations with or how frequently you screwed your better half? Goodbye!

I turned on my side on the bed and confronted the wall away from him. Minutes later, I felt his hands on me. He delicately turned me around. He started saying 'sorry' He maintained his affection for me. He kissed me. His lips made a trip down to my areolas; he sucked them. He was unpleasant, gnawing and crushing my delicate skin. He sucked my dick as well, and his hands ran all around my thighs. His fingers found my poop hole which was at this point to completely contract subsequent to accepting his gigantic dick. He situated himself by stooping toward one side of the bed and hauled me till my midsection was down there, confronting him. Lifting my leg, he mumbled, 'I love your opening, child... I love it... ' And I felt his warm tongue slide inside my butt hole. It dug somewhere inside. Also, he sucked on it. I wriggled and groaned. He came dependent upon me and kissed me generally. And afterward, he began infiltrating me. I felt my opening stretch once more, and I recoiled with some aggravation. His push was wild. I wasn't greased up and the entrance hurt. He push hard a couple of times, prior to pulling out his dick and making me on me feel sick. He lifted my base to his face, and his tongue went in once more. With each stroke of his tongue, he groaned his pleasure. I could feel such a lot of spit fill my butt hole as he tongue-screwed me. Flipping me to my back, he came on top of me, lifted my legs to his shoulders and began stuffing my butt with his stone hard dick. I snatched him tight. He began fucking me. Assuming

full command over me. Squeezing his dick so hard inside me, it felt like he was determined to give me delight I could never get from any other person.
He beat me hard. It hurt. Yet, I invited the agony. I invited the joy as well. I needed this. I needed this man. Furthermore, he needed me as well, since he panted guarantees as he pounded away at me. Vows to be mine. Vows to make me his.

He went at me like a wild canine. I felt like I planned to swoon… his dick was too huge. I had a go at pushing delicately at his midsection, trusting he would comprehend that he expected to dial back. He didn't dial back. He beat until he gave one last snarl and stooped over me as he discharged. Our bodies were smooth with sweat, and our breathing came intensely. He held me to him and murmured, 'You will kill me.'

I grinned with profound delight at that. Obviously, I wouldn't kill him. I essentially believed him should continue to do this to me again and again.

Do you realize you have not delivered, he abruptly said.

Indeed, yet I'm here to satisfy you, I answered.

No, no, no… you need to deliver. Let me know what I ought to do. He was determined.

I advised him to wank me and suck my areolas. He did this, and bit by bit, the surge of semen gathered speed inside my crotch. I hardened and extended my legs as the energy went up the length of my dick. Furthermore, after a second, I was shooting out my heap, moaning with delight as I did that. I was shocked and attempting to relax. Furthermore, I was far spent, positively. Akpan maneuvered me into his arms, inquired as to whether I cherished him, and when I said OK, we at long last surrendered to rest.

That was the manner by which my relationship with Akpan began. We continued with our sexual relationship, getting together for energetic snare ups whenever we found the opportunity. He turned out to be very possessive and over-sexed. My butt truly required a break from his various and energetic fucking. He was fixated and stunned with me. It felt consoling, to have him feel so energetically about me.

My folks were separated and didn't live in a similar state. Despite the fact that I remained with my mom, at times, I visited my dad. What's more, when I completed my tests for that term, I went to remain for quite a while with my dad.

After fourteen days, I was back. I didn't seen Akpan for quite a while after I returned, which was uncommon. I asked after him, and discovered that the property manager's better half blamed him for something deplorable, which brought about him getting terminated. From what I assembled from the talk factory, she'd been keen on him physically. What's more, he repelled her advances. A cutting edge rendition of Joseph and Potiphar's significant other's story. Following the end of his business, he got back to his town.

The news disheartened me. For a really long time, I was exceptionally discouraged. I was unable to contact him, and gradually, I understood that the farewell I shared with him before I left for my dad's home was the final I could at any point see him. I supplicated then, as I actually do, that he will make love and progress any place he is, on the grounds that he is somebody who merits it.

CHAPTER 4

My high school lover

I had a great deal of trouble with my schooling in light of the fact that my dad's work continued to move him starting with one spot then onto the next and that made me rehash classes a ton.

I selected into another school and ended up being one of the most seasoned male in the school (there were three of us who were of a similar age range). However, among us three, I looked the most seasoned in light of the fact that I developed pretty quick. Because of qualities. Indeed, even at north of 6 feet, I previously had heaps of facial and chest hair and was completely evolved. I neither stuck around my schoolmates nor made companions. Not Because I was more seasoned or a censure but since I was a self observer and a man of not many words.

In my inn, there was a person called Julius whom we scratch named "Julius Begger". This was on the grounds that Julius Begged alot. He generally appeared to be In some need. Something else about Julius was that he was a naughtiness. He was attached to continuously telling messy sexual wisecracks (the greater part of them on homosexuality) and that's what I loathed. He was likewise enamored with contacting folks on their confidential part and taking off.

Julius was smallish In height, very gorgeous And exceptionally brilliant. He was the library regent and had a seriously decent handle of information. Julius was likewise attached to Nick naming individuals and I wasn't saved. He referred to me as "father gorilla" (cos of my immense shaggy height) and it stuck like paste.

One night, I had recently cleaned up in the lodging and was at my storage attempting to saturate my body when Julius accompanied a cup asking for milk. He was butt exposed (one more standard In same-sex residence). He kidded about extending to any individual who offered him milk a blow employment chance and everybody chuckled.

"father gorilla you sef shake body little nah...don't be parsimonious " he shared with me.

As I advised him to get into some dresses, Julius, with the speed of a feline, snatched my dick and dashed for the entryway.

" JESU OOOOO!!!!"
he shouted.

"Daddy gorilla prick na ruler Kong.....my God!!!! Which kain prick you get? What's more, the tin won't ever stand" . He looked truly amazed at my dick.

Valid; My dick is way over your standard "enormous dick" And even at that age, it had completely evolved like the remainder of my body.

At that point, the main young lady I have endeavored to fuck was my ministers little girl however she had serious trouble taking me and consistently griped about torments.

"the Kain style wey go fit Papa gorilla prick na monkey style o" he said jokingly.

I was so humiliated.

"Once more, which one be monkey style?"

a lodging mate asked Julius.

"show us...make we see the style"

someone else inquired.

Julius being his standard self, didn't hold back. He dropped his cup, laid on the inn floor, swung his legs with such simple adaptability that his the two feet locked behind his head. He currently separated his butt with two hands uncovering the redness of his man opening.

"father gorilla....papa gorilla....ahhhhhssshhhh....oohh.....aaahhh screw me" he groaned as he copied getting ass screwed.

"unresolved issue (a shoptalk for homosexuality) " the entire lodging sneered at him.

The reality was that no one took Julius serious. He was simply doing his typical trash and that was great diversion.

Be that as it may, something truly weird happened.

As I watched him take that position and saw his opening, my dick expanded with programmed retaliation. I promptly convoluted and squeezed my dick so severe with my storage so no one would take note. I constrained myself to eliminate the image of his opening from my brain however it was unimaginable.

I looked again at him and despite the fact that he had stood up, he had a kind of thoroughly search in his eyes that caused me to feel he realized I was turned on.

I started breathing so particularly weighty as I squashed my dick on my storage while claiming to be going through my pack. I probably been squeezing my dick so hard on the grounds that unexpectedly, I felt hot cum overflow out from my enlarged prick and wetting my thighs. Notwithstanding my large towel I can't help thinking about what my inn mates would agree assuming that they saw sperm dropping on the floor.

"daddy gorilla abeg nah" Julius was presently in a real sense behind me. I just stuck my hand into my pack and provided him with my entire tin of controlled milk.

"everything????" He inquired

"indeed. Simply take it and go" I said discourteously attempting to excuse him. My towel was absorbed with cum and the last thing I needed was to be gotten.

"igweeeeee!!!!" he hailed as he prostrated before me. "no psyche these miserly individuals" he expressed; Refering to other inn folks . "no concern I go give you nyash fuck" he said as he investigated my eyes and grinned. My dick started expanding frantically once more and I immediately went to do my unfortunate acting with my pack.

Since that day, I couldn't say whether I was following Julius or he was following me since we appeared to be in a similar spot simultaneously in any event, during school hours. We never let out the slightest peep to one another. Simply eye to eye connection.

One evening, there was a weighty deluge and the entire lodging was in obscurity because of the blackout. Understudies (myself comprehensive) where bringing precipitation water pouring from the rooftop in their containers.
There was a brilliant blaze of easing up and right then and there, I got Julius remaining at the opposite finish of the deck region checking me out. My heart skipped. The inn as well as the porch region was exceptionally uproarious from understudies which seemed like shadows in the chilly evening contending and singing under the stunning thunder of the downpour. I could see the shadow of Julius go into the lodging through the entry near him and not long after he showed up.

Julius didn't check me out. He basically strolled into the downpour and appeared to gradually evaporate into the weighty deluge. Call it nature or reflex activities yet I realized I needed to follow him. As I ventured into the virus downpour, my eyes never left the shadow that was meandering further into the virus wet evening.

My head shouted "return" however I knew for sure moving ahead was the only option. My feet presently had their very own brain and with each step I took, the commotion from the inn appeared to blur. The downpour drops felt like sharp needles on my skin as the sky streaked with blinding easing up and seethed with thunder. My feet weren't the main thing in my body that had a brain of their own...my dick was currently completely erect (pass to the picture of his man twat that was as yet inked in my mind) and was charged to the point that I had to grasp it to prevent it from tearing itself out of my body and running in front of me.

As I strolled, all there was ; was the cadence of my shoes on the wet mud, the pounding of my heart in my chest and the downpour.

At the point when I saw the shadow make a transform and out of nowhere vanished into a corner, it occurred to me where I was. I was remaining before the school library which was very nearly a 12 minutes stroll from the inn. It seemed like I magically transported or did an evaporating stunt to get to my area since I could swear it was basically impossible that I could cover such distance in what felt like seconds.

Drenched to my bones with a dick of steel , I ventured into the dim library like a hunter prepared to track down its prey. Yet again there was a brilliant glimmer of easing up from the sky god and the entire library was lit with blinding white yellow light. Right away, I saw him. Resting on a work area on couple of meters from me.

I pivoted, shot the entryway and advanced towards him. At the point when I got to where he was, I recently stood. Feet stuck to the floor with a firm chicken previously gesturing in my shorts. In the obscurity I could make out his blameless grin. Despite the fact that the entire library reverberated with the downpour which was falling on its zinc rooftop, it seemed like my heart beat was the most intense.

"what's going on?" Julius asked me with a grin. I didn't answer him. His virus hands started touching my wide bushy chest through my wet singlet and met my areolas. Gradually, he put his hands under my singlet and felt my uncovered body. As he feather contacted my body, it made me tickle however I smothered my chuckle since I was frozen.

"WHAT ARE YOU DOING?????" My head shouted at me once more. "Instruct HIM TO STOP!!!"

Julius gravitated toward to me and appeared to remain on his toes as he tried to kiss me. He put his tongue in my mouth and brought my hands round his delicate body. I let it hang freely on the grounds that was a frightened. In any case, sooner or later, I then I thought to myself....."fuck dread". After this what I needed. For this reason I followed him.

I kissed him back. Sucked and licked his mouth frantically. I held him tight in a decent press and liftedhim to sit on the work area he was resting on. His mouth found my areolas and my head swam with joy. Taking every one of my areolas in a steady progression, his tongue satisfied me in manners I was unable to envision.

He delicately attracted my head down to his areolas and I gave up the entirety of my mouth brought to the table. I sucked , licked and bit his areolas. He got my hair and groaned. I removed his shorts and went for his dick. I took his dick in my mouth and sucked them the most effective way I could and afterward , he brought his advantages in a way I was up close and personal with his butt hole.

There was a blaze of easing up. Indeed, even the sky needed to make a snap effort of that superb opening. I didn't stand by to think. I just went for his poop hole. I sucked it like my endurance in life was inside his opening.

"finger me daddy gorilla" he groaned. He didn't have to ask two times. I licked my finger and pulled out all the stops. I stuck my huge fingers into his tight opening as Our lips met by and by.

This time, kissing more profound than any other time in recent memory.

As I finger screwed him, he held my wrist and eliminated my hand from his opening. He carried my finger to his mouth and sucked on them and afterward drove it back to his opening again.

I was so surprised. My dick went wild with franticness.

I have never seen such freakiness.

I promptly stuck to this same pattern. I stuck my finger into his opening and ensured I pushed it so profound. I brought it out and tasted my finger.

It was a piece sharp yet I wouldn't fret. I took the plunge once more. This time I utilized two fingers. Julius curved his back in torment however with one hand I held the little of his back to keep him set up. I pulled out and sucked my two huge fingers ravenously.

I kept kissing him as I finger screwed him when I saw the smell of child oil. I felt his hands on my over size prick scouring it up with child oil. He started giving me access to his space yet I was eager. I situated myself and started to lead the pack by pushing into him. He shouted and needed to drive me away yet it was past the point of no return. I held his abdomen and was resolved achieved my main goal. The entire of my really thick 10 inches was currently practically inside him.

I have felt nothing so exceptionally enormous as the caring warm hug of his poop hole on my dick. He shouted so clearly yet the weighty deluge on the rooftop suffocated his shout. He took a stab at pulling me away from him yet I was unable to let him. I started beseeching him and kissing him to quiet him down. Fortunately, he loose and permitted me proceed.

The more I screwed him, the more it appeared to be his poop hole was getting wet cos it felt so damp and sweet. I pushed my dick more profound until it was totally lost in his honey pot. I believed I could swoon from this glorious pleasantness. "fuck me.....fuck me please...oh screw me" he beseeched me.

Hearing him ask for my dick started up my bones. I started to mallet and hitter his opening as though I was satisfying an exceptional predetermination and from his groans, I realized he was cherishing it.

Julius dick was in the middle between our stomach and as we screwed, the grating of our stomach appeared to give him delight. Julius started to groan truly clearly and afterward I felt a great deal of wetness on my stomach as his butt muscles pressed my chicken so hard. I had zero control over mypush and before I realized what was occurring , I felt my sperm getting away from like a stream into his opening. It felt so extraordinarily smooth and sweet that I just held him close and took a stab at pausing to rest.

"the number of individuals that have you done this with?" we asked at the same time. We both snickered at ourselves. I let him know nobody and admitted he was my most memorable same-sex insight however he didn't trust me. Julius referenced two names and let me know they use to be seniors however had graduated. I was so envious. The prospect of somebody fucking his sweet ass was simply too excruciating to even consider envisioning. As I attempted to pull out myself from him, Julius pulled me back to him and locked his legs around my abdomen.

"wetin dey concern you sef?......no do at any rate before you hack slap now" he said as he energetically slapped my cheek. I was at that point succumbing to him. This little person that I could smash with one hand having such a loud mouth was truly fascinating. I just checked out at him and shook my head. The downpour had died down thus had the reverberation. In the dimness of the library , myself standing handle stripped and Julius half sitting on the work area actually having my semi erect rooster in his opening, his hands round my neck and mine round his abdomen, we both realized there was something unique that had started.

We started talking.

He inquired as to why I was still in optional school at my age and I educated him regarding my dad's profession as well as other individual family matters. Julius trusted in me and enlightened me regarding his mum who was a unimportant dealer and was battling to get by. His father had left his mom and nobody knew his whereabouts.

As we unburdened out hearts to one another, Julius started to stroke my chest hair and areolas and I could feel my rooster extend inside his cum splashed opening. "awful nigger" he groaned into my ears and grinned. I was unable to help myself. I began fucking him once more. In any case, this time it was anything but a distraught unpleasant sex as I did previously. This time I went slow. I took as much time as necessary to partake in the pleasantness of him as well as taste his lips. It was genuine sorcery. No sooner, I felt my cum develop and absolved his opening with new sperm. I was spent.

We kissed and snuggled. I didn't have any idea how long we remained in the library yet I realized the time had come to return to the inn. As I pulled out my dick from him, I needed to utilize my singlet to clean my clammy dick yet he halted me. Descending from the work area, he went kneeling down and cleaned my dick with his tongue. I was so dazzled I needed to kiss him with appreciation.
EWe advanced back to inn and when we showed up, it was truly dull and each one had hit the hay. I got on my bonk and set down. My dick began rising again on the grounds that I was aware of my experience with Julius. I was unable to accept how a man's butt could be so sweet.

As I constrained myself to rest, I felt a hand contact me. It was Julius. I was apprehensive yet I moved for himself and he laid on my bunk. The lodging was in pitch haziness so I was sure nobody could see us.

"go to the floor" I murmured in his ear and he complied. I spat on all fours it on my rooster and his poop hole. I unobtrusively laid on his back as he directed me into him. His opening was as yet wet from the two gallons of sperm I stored in him.

I was so dazzled the way that my thick dick could enter him no sweat. We unobtrusively screwed and I discreetly came. He left for his bed and I crawled into mine.

Everybody was astounded at our abrupt closeness and could never have a clarification for it since it appeared to come about pretty much by accident. We went to class together and returned to the inn together.

We became indistinguishable until we completed auxiliary school and got into the equivalent university.

CHAPTER 5

Relationship between me and my aunty's husband

In the mid 90s I lived with my auntie; pamella in ikoyi. Regardless of she was intended to be my gatekeeper, she was mean and horrendous as Satan might at any point be.

My mum, who tragically became a single parent (on the grounds that popsi left us matter-of-factly) chose to return to school in the UK.

She as a rule sends me cash through my auntie and sometimes, my aunt will send my mum photographs of me looking fashionable and folding my legs in her living room with her grinning cheerfully with me; when truly, I was hopeless and wasn't permitted to try and sit on her couch or eat from her China products (the vast majority of which had a place with my mum).

In the road where we resided, my auntie was the serious deal . She was a general public woman and was what you could depict as "yellow sisi" (all from fading). She had 4 vehicles. A Mercedes benz, Daewoo racer, santana and 504. Which were all high profile vehicles in the mid 90's.

She had shops and a Boutiques spread all over Lagos however the flashy way of life she lived was certainly not simply from her organizations.

Aunt Pamela had a spouse (uncle Gbemiga) who was continually battling with her. He was Tall, attractive and thin. His look helped me to remember men during the 70s you find in high contrast photographs.

Afro hair, athletic form and a thick side consumes that prompted a similarly thick mustache. Uncle Gbemiga was more youthful than my auntie and like me, was similarly treated as a slave. Each time he contended with aunt Pamela, she never neglected to remind him who "gave him a day to day existence".

He was articulate, instructed and exceptionally shrewd. Now and then I asked why he for sure didn't have a unique kind of energy. He dealt with her business and was continually blamed for being a cheat. My auntie had 2 youngsters and talk had it that they were not Gbemiga's . I previously thought it was only nature's blunder that the children turned out monstrous until I saw aunt Pamela's friendly benefactor. He was the spit duplicate of the children. He was fat and past monstrous. He seemed to be your commonplace wizard in Nollywood films.

Clearly, he was the significant margarine on aunt Pamela's bread and whenever he came around the house, myself and Gbemiga turned out to be essentially imperceptible. If he somehow happened to go through the evening, Gbemiga will go along with me in the young men quarter until he left. The main time he (Gbemiga) had a daily existence or was permitted in the image was when aunt Pamela had an occasion to join in and required a human accomplice to display for society.

Something beneficial was that aunt Pamela was not really around so we (myself and Gbemiga) had the house to ourselves. We were brilliant not to exploit what is going on the grounds that on a few events, she had shown up startlingly at odd hours. Clearly expecting to find us involving her home for something horrible.
Among the things I heard was that Gbemiga once lived in Akwa-ibom state and had great capabilities. His mom (who died) use to be aunt Pamela's companion. Aunt Pamela had guaranteed paradise and earth to Gbemiga provided that he would move to Lagos and deal with her organizations. As time went on, aunt Pamela made a deal that they go into an organized marriage since she was stressed over what individuals will say assuming that they found she was pregnant without both mom and dad present (thusly making the reports about my cousin's dad valid). She likewise never permitted Gbemiga keep any relationship with another lady despite the fact that they concurred he was allowed to do his thing. She started requesting intimate ceremonies from him which was breaking their understanding. Gbemiga blamed her for utilizing juju (voodoo) on him. Throughout the yelling and contention, Gbemiga told Pamela she was nothing without him; and this; I accepted.

Pamela didn't possess the brainpower for carrying on with work and Gbemiga ran everything for her.

I was still in tears when he came into my room and attempted to comfort me. He embraced me and scoured my back advising me to relax. Despite the fact that I was genuinely destroyed, I really wanted to see the vibe his dick on my body as we remained in a hug. I professed to cry some more so we could stay there for somewhat more longer. That evening, I dozed in his arms with my back to him with Our exposed topless living, breathing people embracing.

Uncle Gbemiga in the end moved into my room and that is the manner by which we became flat mates.

At some point, I awakened alone and it appeared Gbemiga was out. He returned right away with breakfast which he ate. Aunt Pamela was out however gotten back without further ado. She came to the young men quarter (something she doesn't do) and got some information about certain provisions. She likewise requested that he go to one of her shops to convey a few things however Gbemiga told her that he had different plans and will carry on with work later. Her eyes became red with outrage yet she attempted to oversee herself. She asked where he was going to and he told her he was taking me out. "who will be in the house?" she inquired. The look Gbemiga gave her was sufficient.

"If it's not too much trouble, attempt to return on time" was all she said as she left. I told Gbemiga we ought to delay the excursion however he demanded we go. While heading to the ocean side, we halted at an office complex and got a young lady. She was pretty and youthful. I was desirous to such an extent that I would not talk. Gbemiga presented me as his nearby more youthful sibling. He continued to take a gander at me from the back reflect and probably saw my face.

At the point when we got to the ocean side, Gbemiga was truly playing straightforwardly with this young lady to the point he had a weighty erection which I saw from under the table while we sat in a bar. His dick was very lengthy. It appeared as though it was nearly getting to his knees.

I was moved by it as I recently featured. I didn't focus on anything they were saying yet it was the young ladies giggle that definitely stood out and made me turn upward. Despite the fact that I didn't have the foggiest idea what the young lady said, I could perceive Gbemiga was truly annoyed. She didn't appear to mind a lot. She continued tasting her fanta and gesturing to the sound of shina Peters coming from the bar.

There was a long quietness and she viewed at my face as though doing an investigation. Taking a gander at my nails, she then inquired "what is on your nails?....are you a young lady?" (alluding to my well self manicured and cleaned nail).

As a disturbed youth, I have created metal skin and in addition to the fact that i was skilled to see conceal; I knew how to remove any tree that gave it. Curving a forehead, I answered "what is on my nails? You're a lady. You ought to understand what it is...".

As I expected, she didn't see it coming. Clearly she felt offended and said "resembles you need home preparation". As she talked, she utilized her straw to sprinkle the remenant drops of fanta all over.

Gbemiga's eyes and mouth opened wide with shock. So enraged, I stood up and sprinkled what was left in my glass all over. I was prepared for a battle.

She had a go at going after her shoes (clearly to toss it on me). Right now, Gbemiga was making an honest effort to stop what is happening. She tossed her shoes at me and I dodged. She went after Gbemiga's jug and that was the point at which I immediately utilized the table to push her to the floor. As

I progressed towards her, Gbemiga got me and pulled ME away rapidly. Yet, he was excessively late. I kicked a lot of sand towards her that arrived on her head and face.

"are you distraught?" Gbemiga murmured at me and out of nowhere white light glimmered in my eye as my cheek stung. He slapped me. With my hand on my cheek, I froze. I could see a touch of frenzy shrouded in statement of regret all over.

His visitor started to swear at me and Gbemiga cautioned her to quiet down. However, she didn't. "you began this mess....why did you sprinkle a beverage all over?" Gbemiga asked her while attempting to protect me.

"futile Man. Is there any valid reason why you won't side him? Come and fuck toto let God rebuff you" she shouted like a frantic lady.

Little groups started to assemble and Gbemiga requested me to begin going towards the vehicle. I could hear her shouting as I strolled to the vehicle leave. Few moments later Gbemiga went along with me and we drove home.
"am finished with them. Useless piece of shit.....All of them!!!!!" he reviled softly. I actually claimed to be in torment as I bowed my head and held my cheek.

"sorry about that" he said as he went after my thighs and presses them to help his conciliatory sentiment. I didn't move nor say a word.

When we returned home, I hit the hay and confronted the wall. As I wailed quietly, I could feel strain on the bed as though somebody had plunked down adjacent to me. "chu"- (a pet name he'd given me) he called. I didn't answer. I experienced the glow of his huge palms on my back as he started to stroke it delicately. Once more he was sorry and kidded that assuming I keep on crying, he also would go along with me. I grinned to myself but since my face was to the wall, he was unable to see me. "chu" he called once more. "for what reason are you doing this naw?" He asked with enthusiasm in his voice. His hand was still on my back. Gbemiga who was currently laying alongside me started imitating a terrible sobbing cry that constrained me to snicker.
I turned over into his arms as nestled me hidden from everyone else. He was sorry again and we both started talking. I prodded him about the young lady whom I, first of all, had a fight with. He had a go at shielding himself saying she wasn't his sort and that all he really wanted was a shag. He requested me what sort from young lady I liked and in the event that I had a young lady companion. I let him know I wasn't actually into young ladies and he snickered saying "I know". He let me know it was to my benefit and I ought to save it that way however long I would be able. He said all ladies are wired something similar and everything necessary is for one occurrence to uncover their real essence. He made a reference to aunt Pamela and how he thought she was overall quite confided in her. We additionally discussed the little we could recollect about what it seemed like having a mother which was very personal for the two of us

What amazed me was that while We talked , I had my hands inside his shirt tenderly stroking his chest hair while he inactively stroked my shoulder. I thought he was turned on however there was no indication of erection on the shorts he wore. As my hands made a trip to his stomach and contacted his paunch button his breath changed. Directly in front of me I watched his dick rise like a monster mixing from its sleep.

Appeared he saw he was getting turned on the grounds that he tried to hide his developing penis and dis-connect with himself from our snuggling. I immediately went after his dick before he prevailed with regards to taking care of it however he got my hand and we both started a fun loving battle. He wanted two hands to hold his erection so it offered me the chance to begin stimulating him as well as contact his stomach button more.

"chu what Is it nah??...." He argued as he giggled madly.

"show me something jare" I requested as I continued tickling and battling for his gut button and dick.

"isn't it exactly the same thing you have?" He inquired.

"says Who? ...How might you contrast a tooth pick with a tuber of sweet potato?" I answered.

Gbemiga snickered so hard at my explanation that tears moved down his eyes.

At the point when he saw that attempting to persuade me to disregard his dick and quit stimulating him wasn't working, he had no real option except to give up. His dick was presently limp yet looked weighty with guaranteeing guarantees. I saw it, held it and as It rose as I petted it, he halted me sufficiently saying...."That's".

From that day, myself and Gbemiga's bond established. We started showering together and nestling consistently to rest. He currently started allowing me to play with his paunch button while we sat in front of the TV or recently loose. In some cases I will place my hand in his fighters and contact his dick and he will not do or say anything. I surmise he was totally gullible about same sex guilty pleasure cos whenever I get stirred when we shower , he will ask me for what good reason am being turned on and we will simply snicker.

at the point when we shower , he will ask me for what reason am being turned on and we will simply snicker.

One night it came down intensely and aunt Pamela was away. Myself and Gbemiga laid in one another's arms as we rested. One thing about Gbemiga is that he can be an exceptionally weighty sleeper. Right now I had arrived at my desire limit for his thick and long rooster. I eliminated myself from his hug and turned on the light. I delicately turned him over to his back and I could see the print of his weighty dick lying on laps. No big surprise aunt Pamela was ravenous.

I started stroking his dick and brought it out from the edge of his fighters. I stuffed my mouth with his 12+ inches dark dick and each time I constrained it more profound into my throat, his breathing became further and his rooster pulsated wrathfully in my mouth. I severely needed to take his dick in my butt and I knew whether I continued to suck , he would cum from my A1 sucking abilities.

I got my butt greased up as well as his dick. Switching off the light, I peeled off my garments and continued my resting position however this time, with my exposed air pocket butt and his boa constrictor appropriately greased up.

Raising one of my leg, I pointed his exceptionally large penis at my eager opening and gradually directed him into me. Delicately and persistently , I figured out how to fit his tremendous snake into my stove. I started fucking his dick quite simple when he snorted and nestled me closer. He pushed lethargically. I stopped. After few seconds I kept fucking his chicken sideways style while I wanked myself.

"chu what are you doing????" He asked me.

I was frozen as My heart whipped stunningly in my chest like a distraught confined lion.

"goodness my God!!!" he wheezed as he split away from me and immediately made for the light switch. When the room was splendid , he seen his actually erect clammy dick and at me with complete grave unbelief.

"was I fucking you a few seconds ago?" He asked ; trusting I would agree no.

All I did was grin and feign exacerbation like I normally do to him at whatever point he wasn't seeming to be OK.

"Chuka!!! .....Am serious!!!! ......Answer me!!!!"

"OK yes...yes....i have responded to you. Are you fulfilled now?" I answered peevishly as I made for my garments. Gbemiga sank to the floor and continued to mumble "I don't trust it" as he shut his eyes and raised his head up.

"Am grieved" I said.

He didn't answer me.

"I will begin crying o" I prodded as I sat on the floor close to him. I started to copy his example of crying he did whenever I was vexed. Gbemiga grinned and covered his face with his enormous palms.

"chu it's not funny....please don't try again later"

"I can't guarantee you that dear" I said as I rested on him and stroked his head.

I knew for specific he won't drive me away. Gbemiga cherished me to say the least and I realized he was sex starved. In particular, I realized he partook in my succulent opening and couldn't completely accept that my poop hole was equipped for obliging his enormous masculinity.

"return to the bed" I encouraged him as I held his hands and pulled him up to his feet. As he hesitantly stood up, I embraced him and pecked his cheeks. Gbemiga was the kind of man who had a gigantic soft spot for straightforward presentation of friendship and I gave him excess of that.

I realized he was not generally annoyed with me

While we returned to bed, I cuddled dependent upon him and started letting him know How much he intended to me. He as well, let me know what I provided him motivation to mean for a day to day existence. while we talked, my hands never left his gut button and he didn't hinder me. His dick was as yet erect however we both gave no consideration to it as we talked.

"didn't it torment you ?" He asked timidly.

"didn't what torment me?" I asked teasingly. "say the name jor"

"you're spoilt." He snickered. " Okay...fine...fine...its my dick. Didn't my dick torment you?" He asked timidly.

"isn't love torment?" I answered; as I went after his solid enormous cassava.

"chu-chu.....please nawwww....stop" he beseeched me. " you're not a young lady now....this is some way or another"

"There is no in some way jor. You're talking as though you don't adore me anymore....as in the event that you didn't appreciate chuking your large penis in my butt hole" I answered as I got rid of my garments and got ontop of him.

"chu-chu...you have begun again o.....what are you doing?" He asked tediously.

"Am completing what I began furthermore this monster needs to take care of". I said as I kneaded his currently enlarged prick.

Gbemiga just tossed his head in reverse and continued to murmur "kindly stop this". Yet, it was past the point of no return. Past the point of no return. I had proactively drawn out his rooster, spat on my hand and yet again soaked my yet to differentiate opening as well as his fat prick.

I started pushing down myself down on him and as I sank down, he groaned so quietly that it emerged as an odd music note. I began riding him however he just laid still. Didn't contact nor push "uncle Gbemiga kindly screw me" I beseeched him truly. He just laid still and stayed quiet. He wasn't answering and it seemed like I was constraining him.

I got off him and confronted the wall. "goodbye" I said forcefully.

"what is it again now chu?" He inquired.

"it resembles am upsetting your life and driving my adoration on you....so I rather mind my own business"
"however, I permitted you would what you like to do naw....Didn't I?" He sounded befuddled and a piece frantic.

I didn't respond to him. I just laid still.

"what is it that you need ?" he inquired.

"You heard what I mentioned" I said.

"okay...as you wish. However, am doing this to satisfy you" he said.

I pivoted and met his attractive face peering down on me. I contacted his facial hair, neck and his areolas. He realized I cherished him and I was certain He was as well.

"I have not done this before chu-chu"...he attempted to say ....as I feigned exacerbation and had a go at confronting the wall once more, he halted me.

"try not to betray me chu" he argued yet at the same time made it sound like an admonition.

He got on top of me, raised my the two advantages and had a go at finding himself mixed up with me. It was agonizing cos my spit had dried from his dick so I needed to stop him and once again saturated both hardware. When he got each centimeter of his palm tree into me, we both investigated each other's eyes and at the same time we grinned.

"what's entertaining you ?" we asked all the while. We both giggled and afterward he pushed areas of strength for so me that it made me jerk and wheeze.

"you like it? .....is this what you need?" He asked me as he push himself into me once more. This time, harder than the first.

I couldn't resist the opportunity to groan "goodness yes" in sweet distress.

He situated himself appropriately and got fucking the thunder going my butt. I pulled out all the stops as I shouted and ripped at his back with my nails. He recoiled in torment from my nails attacking the tissue on his back and went after my two hands. His two hands held down both of my hands as he investigated my eyes with serious power; beating and dissipating my butt as he continued to inquire "is this the very thing you need?"

Despite the fact that I felt my butt hole consume from his thorough pushing, I didn't believe he should stop. I could see He was cherishing each snapshot of it from his looks. He preferred seeing he was scoring his focuses and that by itself made my dick so rock hard that as he held me down and destroyed my walls, hot sperm shot out of my dick and sprinkled on his stomach and chest. He dialed back and watched in wonder as my dick discharge thick white smooth sperm. As I investigated his eyes , I could see He had tracked down another sort pleasantness and without a doubt, he was cherishing each and every piece.

His pushing expanded irately as his eyes continued to shoot between my sperm stained dick and face. The pushing was areas of strength for so felt my cum developing once more. He began to groan and quickly I went along with him. Sperm started shooting by and by from my dick and I could feel a progression of warm water falls flood inside my opening. I could swear he came. My opening was throbbing close by his monstrous prick and we both were gasping as though we had ran an Olympic long distance race.

I rolled and angled my midriff while crushing his dick with my extremely splashed butt hole. He shivered and gradually continued to screw me.

"you preferred that don't you?" He inquired.

"so much.....i need more" I groaned.

"That is my chu" he groaned.

"turn your back and curve down.....am not done at this point" he murmured in my ears and to my suprise , he kissed me completely on the lips however concise, it was profound and exotic.

As he pulled out his dick from my battered opening , I looked with stand amazed at the still erect dick that remained before me. It was so long....so thick.....full of veins....from the cap of his dick to the base was exceptionally thick. He was an affirmed steed with unique pull. I grinned with reverence and he grinned back at me.

Without with nothing to do, I laid level on my stomach. As I set my butt high up in the air, I heard him groan "yes child" and afterward I felt his snake attack my Eden. In a real sense I was tolerating him and needed to shout into the cushion in light of the fact that the sensation was horrendous for me. Another fucking meeting started. He was going for his second round immediately.

This time around he was delicate and took as much time as necessary. I began stroking my dick to redirect the thrilling desolation my twat was experiencing the position.

"might you at any point screw me ordinary ?" I inquired.

"do you need me to?......i can ; assuming that is owhat you need". He murmured in my ears.

"I need to be your sweetheart. I believe you should fuck me....fuck me in light of the fact that am yours." I recently continued to say various kinds and he continued to answer "uunnn hunnnnn".

My opening was completely exhausted and started releasing ass squeeze that made extremely clearly slurpy sounds as he slammed into me without kindness. I had become so free and additional wet that Gbemiga's dick had definitely no doubts to venture into any secret chambers in my butt.

He started snorting and jolting as He released cluster 2 cum in my generally abused opening.

To say I was depleted was a finished misrepresentation of reality. I came 3x in the subsequent round and 2x in the main round making it a sum of 5. Gbemiga shot 2x however had the effect of 10 rounds.

From that day onwards, Gbemiga strictly screwed me ordinarily for quite a while that extended into years.

CHAPTER 6

THE UNEXPECTED TWITTER SCANDAL

I have this distraught sexually open sweetheart whose name is favor. She is petit and had a body and face That could make holy messengers tumble from paradise in their thousands.

Asides her enchanting looks, she isn't your typical lady when it came to insight. She was free, monetarily got and has a life partner who was really hot; a global dealer and loves her to bits. He realized she was sexually unbiased and was cool with it . Favor was exceptionally faithful to him and won't ever undermine him regardless of how much abundance was hung before her.

The main issue with favor was her naughtiness. She would open a few catfish account on Facebook and Twitter just to prod folks and request their bare photographs and recordings for no particular reason. Since She realized I cherished taking a gander at such, she continued providing me with mouth watering materials. Subsequent to drawing these Randy men (for the most part hitched) and getting them snared , she will unexpectedly impede or erase them for not a great explanation. At times she will go similar to addressing them on the telephone (utilizing a SIM card exclusively for such purposes) and putting it on speaker for me to tune in as they wanked while saying every conceivable kind of irreverence to her.

Notwithstanding the way in which insane she went, she never met them face to face , gave her own contact or sent her genuine photographs.

On one occasion I was working when favor called me. The principal thing she said was "yawa wear gas o... abeg find corner make I brief you sharp ". I was a piece frightened in light of the fact that I could detect inconvenience. Ordinarily, Anytime she requests that I head off to some place segregated for a conversation, it implied inconvenience. I immediately went into the workplace latrine to talk.

Favor was terrifying as she started informing me concerning one of the ones who she had met through her catfish account that professed to be a tactical staff had found her. She informed me that as she addressed me, he was hanging tight for her external her office.

Since I knew every one of her manikins, it was easy to know the individual she was discussing once she let me know what its identity was. His name Is chukwuma yet we had nicknamed him "significant burden champion" cos of his construct and furthermore huge dick. Despite the fact that he's simply in his late 20s, He looked way experienced for his age and damn excessively attractive. Amazingly, he was one (in the event that not by any means the only one) of the not many who had denied abandoning correspondence regardless of how discourteous blessing was; Unlike the other people who developed cold feet once favor began getting cold or gave demeanor. He was dependably quiet and incredibly understanding. I truly enjoyed his personality (and dick as well).

Favor let me know she went to shoprite to purchase lunch and in light of the fact that there was a line, she inactively started going through her Twitter catfish account when out of nowhere, the telephone which had the catfish SIM card started to ring. She saw who the guest was nevertheless overlooked it since she wasn't in that frame of mind for senseless discussions. Be that as it may, the telephone continued to ring free until she had to turn it off.

"you ought to answer your telephone" a voice said behind her. Pondering who the rubberneck was, she pivoted exclusively to perceive the face featuring back at her. Her reflex activities quickly sold her spot on as "chukwuma!!!!" spilled from her lips. Obviously , he was behind her the entire time and saw her Twitter account which he perceived.

She let me know he had requested clarifications over her games and she needed to lie that her gay sibling is the first proprietor of the record but since of the apprehension about disgrace, he claims to be female so he could have the chance to visit with folks. She further made sense of that the calls was only her approach to concealing for him (her sibling).

"what's more, did he accept?" I asked anxiously.

"that is the reason am calling you nah...he doesn't trust me. I need make you show" she asked.

I was totally lost. I realized something like this will undoubtedly happen one way or the another .

"Officer never beat me and no be today e go occur" I told her point clear.

"na me trooper wear beat abi ? .....abeg no do me this solid thing" she argued.

Presumably myself and favor appeared to be similar and could without much of a stretch pass as kin. We both where a similar level, had the specific skin conceal, enormous front head (like Rhianna) and stammered marginally. Most importantly, we had a similar thought process. Every individual who didn't realize us quickly accepted we where kin.

"we will be coming to pick you from the workplace. Abeg simply stream. Much thanks to you". She said and hung up.

To be sure this was an off-kilter circumstance. I intellectually constrained myself to be quiet. From the little I knew, Chukwuma was a patient man. I wouldn't believe in the event that he ended up being a disturbance... But he was those exceptionally tranquil yet risky sorts.

I investigated my appearance in the reflection of the staff latrine. I wasn't checking full scale. Thank sky I had thorned and shaved not many days prior. I went to ensure my pant fitted great on my huge bum. An enormous piece of me was energized despite the fact that I was anxious.

At around 45minutes later, favor called to tell me they had shown up. I put on some aroma, powdered my face and went down to the vehicle leave. I was still on the telephone as she guided me to the spot they stopped.

Favor was grinning and waving as she remained close to a straightforward Toyota cammery. Right away, my eyes went to the individual sitting on the drivers seat.

WOW!!!!!

The bobo was ravishing. Too ravishing infact. He just gazed directly me as though he was Some kind of examiner. My heart started to pulsate so quick. Not out of dread however out of timidity. I could remember him. I grinned bashfully at him yet all he did was raise his fingers (that grasped the controlling) in affirmation. Favor requested that I get into the vehicle and when I did, I welcomed him appropriately and added "sir". He answered decently and similarly tended to me as "sir" as he kicked turned over the motor.

As we drove, Favor acquainted me with Chukwuma (who continue to look at me through the back reflect) as "her sibling." "the face is there" was his main reaction to the presentation. Favor asked me how was work, chukwuma asked me how I helped a living......after some time, the pressure in me died down and we as a whole (for the most part myself and favor) started talking ceaselessly.

We wound up in a bar and sat at the farthest corner as we started drinking and snacking on nibble. Chukwuma was around for his cousins wedding which was occurring in two days time.

I truly couldn't say whether it was the liquor however Favor truly started flapping her gums. First she discussed how "our folks" tossed me out subsequent to finding my sexuality, how we both needed to assemble our reserve funds to get me a house so I will not be homeless.....lying came out normally from this woman.

"that is truly screwed up. Sorry you needed to go through all that brother". He said. His compassion was certified.

He began conversing with favor (a piece unobtrusively) as though it was a confidential thing. Favor giggled insanely and energetically drove him away. I was puzzled on the grounds that I did not know what was happening.

Pointing at me, she said - "he is the awful one". On the off chance that I could cover myself, I wouldn't hold back the slightest bit since favor began describing not many of my ventures. She discussed a 3some we had with one of her pounds during our optional school days and how I put her; a lady to disgrace. She started adulating my penis massage and getting abilities as though tomorrow had no pertinence.

"FAVOUR!!!!!!" I yelled; expecting to quiet her. Yet, she continued to spill the tea on how great I handle a dick. I turned out to be humiliated to the point that I needed to ask Chukwuma to disregard her.

Shockingly , chukwuma said I ought to be glad as opposed to feel embarrassed.

"you haven't seen anything sef" she said. "allow him to show you".

Getting a medium estimated plastic container water on the table, she held it toward me and said "show your ability".

At some point back , myself and favor saw a photograph of Sam Smith (vocalist) with a plastic jug put as far as possible in his mouth. We found it entertaining and endeavored profound throating a plastic container only for entertainment only. However, she never appeared to prevail at the task...unlike me.

"NO!!!!!!" I said as I become flushed.

"do it jor" chukwuma said with a sprinkle of energy in his voice. Somewhere down in my heart, I realized his endorsement was all I wanted. I just trusted he won't consider me to be a whore.

I took the container and looked at my dearest companion perniciously. "I will kill you for this" I kidded. It took only two push and VOILA!!! The entire jug had vanished leaving simply the base all the rage.

Chukwuma's hands where presently fastened on top of his head with his mouth wide opened in shock. "ooooooo boooooyyyyyy" he shouted in wonderment. Every one of the three of us bursted into giggling. Chukwuma requested me one more jug of wine as a recognition for my expertise.
At the point when the night was very much spent, Favor said she expected to go on the grounds that our mom will be concerned. At the point when the bills came, every one of the three of us requested to pay

exclusively. It was a particularly cordial contention however at long last; as is commonly said,- "never contend with a lady". Favor paid for our beverages.

As we advanced toward the vehicle, Chukwuma asked where he could purchase a decent 3 piece suit...Favour just pointed at me and that was all. Chukwuma argued that I make out time for his shopping the following day since he didn't realize Lagos excessively well and I acknowledged. We dropped off favor and I needed to come to the front seat.

As he drove, he began asking me inquiries for the most part about favor. It appeared he saw as her/our organization fun.

"so do you let each know other everything?" He asked focusing "everything."

"she does...but I don't" I answered.

"why?" He addressed

"since I am a man. That is the reason" was my reaction.

Broadening his huge solid hands he shook me and said - "you are a right man. That's what I love."

It appeared to be my assertion made him more agreeable in light of the fact that he appeared to be more loose.

He asked me the number of folks that have we (myself and favor) had 3some with and I let him know one. He requested that I let him know how it worked out and I did. I let him know how favor had without exception needed to see 2guys make out live and furthermore, at that point, she feared the folks dick and needed help. As I spoke, Chukwuma recently continued to shake his head.

"such an odd family....but I want to believe that you don't screw your sister o" he appeared to compel some humor in his voice. I was wiped out in my stomach from every one of the untruths yet I just figured out how to cooperate.

For some time he was by all accounts in contemplations and afterward he said..."that thing you did with the bottle...." he opened his mouth as though he needed to offer something however at that point shut his mouth.

"what?" I inquired

Once more squinting his face a little, he opened his mouth as though he needed to say something however at that point he shut his mouth and said - "sit back and relax".

We showed up at my place Shortly and traded numbers. I advised him to tell me when shown up his objective since he didn't realize Lagos excessively well and he recently gestured and waved bye.

"Favor has prevailed with regards to destroying my standing just to dispose of a buddy I was pounding on" I contemplated internally.

As I settled down for the evening and about hitting the sack, an instant message came hotel. It was Chukwuma. He'd showed up his objective and said we ought to have a "genuine talk".

At the point when I asked him "what was going on with it?" , he essentially answered "goodnight".

Following day after work , he came to pick me and we Went to get some decent outfit for him. I wound up picking a pleasant Niger Delta outfit for him rather than the 3pc suit as expected. I gave him one of my extravagant clasp which he cherished and he looked truly running. I took several photographs of him while he postured for camera. It was a particularly eminent encounter seeing him present timidly and giggle at himself. I was genuinely succumbing to him however since he was straight and was more into favor, I chose to regard myself and quit wishing.

He requested that I pick the best photograph and show favor. (He was all the while imploring me to converse with her for his benefit). As he dropped me off, he mentioned I went along with him for the wedding and persuade favor to come. I realized favor will deny however to satisfy all uprightness I actually asked her and as I thought , she truly flew off the handle with me for making such ideas.

The next day, I was looking sharp and Chukwuma came to pick me. As we headed to the setting, he began getting some information about what signs to keep an eye out for on the off chance that somebody was gay. I readily addressed all he had to be aware and when I inquired as to whether that was "the discussion" he believed that us should have, he said "NO." He inquired as to whether favor was coming and I let him know I questioned. From his non-verbal communication It appeared he was anticipating that she should turn him down.

The wedding was fun and very ostentatious. Nearly everybody needed to take photographs with Chukwuma along with know where he shops. At the point when it was dance time, Chukwuma took to the floor. He was a particularly horrendous artist but since he couldn't have cared less and was simply doing his thing, he drew alot of consideration and a lot of naira notes where showered on him. I sat at a corner and just respected him; respecting, imaging and wanting to be my sweetheart.

Surprisingly he started moving towards me and this caused alot of to notice me too. He had a go at pulling me up to my feet however I was excessively modest. I'm a generally excellent artist so I just did a few little serious moves that made him (and not many visitor) go "WHHHHOOOOAAAAHHHH!!!!!". I had a go at returning to my seat in the wake of doing my executioner move however out of nowhere I felt his huge hands on my midriff pulling me towards his crotch and started shaking my behind. I nearly entered alarm state of mind (perhaps in light of the fact that I was excessively aware of my sexuality).

I figured out how to move away from his grasp and afterward drew out my telephone from my pocket and started recording him on record as he did his dissipated dance moves happily. He was simply too provocative and cheerful as a kid.

After the party, Chukwuma was a piece blasted however he (and myself) assisted the host with getting together a few things they accompanied. The night was far gone and Chukwuma requested that I spend the night in his lodging while at the same time promising to drop me home prior to making a beeline for Zaria.

At the point when we got to the lodging, he brushed his mouth, had his shower and got into bed. This he managed without saying a word to me. I simply loved seeing him peacefully.

I didn't shower since I have this propensity for continuously utilizing my toiletries or nothing by any means. I additionally didn't perspire as he did so I was great.

Chukwuma requested that I rub his back as he made sense of he's been having back issues. I took some body salve from the table and started dealing with his strong back. He continued mumbling "mhennn much obliged" and two or after three minutes he was wheezing uproariously. I peeled off to my fighters and laid sideways with my butt confronting him in the event he didn't have any idea how to inquire.

Around midnight, I felt his leg rest over me and afterward his body followed.. I laid still; but since his wheezing was still on full stuff, I speculated he knew nothing about what was happening. I attempted to exploit the situation by attempting to snuggle up nearer and crush my hips into his crotch yet the moment I moved, he quit wheezing and said "sorry" and got some distance from me.

Nothing happened any longer and I floated to rest. The following day, as we prepared , he had a go at calling Favor yet she didn't pick his call. He requested that I call her (clearly he was curious as to whether she was keeping away from his calls) yet I rejected. He continued to annoy me and I concurred. Her telephone scarcely rang and the principal thing she said was "significant burden champion wear go?". I turned and viewed at him as I trusted he hadn't heard her. In any case, from his response I realized he did. His shoulders dropped however he figured out how to drive a grin.

I told favor I will get back to her. When I hanged up, he inquired as to whether significant burden champion was the name she gave him and I said OK. He inquired as to why, and I said it was because of his construct. He inquired as to whether he ought to surrender and all I did was gesture. He recently moaned and said - "that is people for you." All I could do was shake my head in understanding.

He dropped me off and we bid farewell. The following day, he called me and let me know he was in Zaria. We talked a little and he said he would re-energize his telephone and get back to me.

Few moments later, he called me and we had a broad discussion. Among the things he said was that "it was miserable he succumbed to some unacceptable individual" (He actually accepted I possessed the record). He asked me how I managed all his bare photographs and I let him know I stroke off with them. He inquired as to for what reason didn't I hush up about my sexuality as opposed to include Favor; I let him know it was on the grounds that I wanted somebody to converse with and favor was the nearest individual to me.

He inquired as to whether I believed that him should screw me the time he welcomed me over to the lodging and requested that I rub his back....I giggled and said "typical thing nah"

His next remark truly irritated me. He presently said - "you appear to be a decent guy....You and your sister. In any case, you are excessively bad and uncovered."

Thank heavens he was back in Zaria so I didn't sit around to release my tongue on him. So I fires back -

"Am not a ho....If that is what you think....just in light of the fact that I realize some stuff doesn't make me some sort of cum cloth. For your data it's getting to 2 years I last engaged in sexual relations. Also, kindly don't pass judgment on my honesty or ethics with my sexual illumination"

"syntax" he answered. "it doesn't eradicate the reality you believed that me should screw your cerebrums out and wash you with my cum like you said on Twitter." He was correct. Those where my definite words. At the point when favor acknowledged I was squashing on him, she generally let me visit with him Whenever he was on the web.

"I can't really accept that I trusted in you...told you individual things without trying seeing you. You generally energized me and spurred me to be better....my never giving up was on the grounds that I thought you had a wrecked life like me and it was you were difficult....I because trusting you will change....I was occupied with falling head over heels not realizing I was cherishing some unacceptable individual. I feel so moronic."

My entire being sank into my stomach as I pondered our visits throughout the long term. We turned out to be near such an extent that he opened dependent upon me like there's no tomorrow. His story was a miserable one. I felt so harmed at one point that favor fended pushing him off and nearly obstructed him if not on the grounds that I had interest in him.

It took a great deal of strain before he consented to send his bare photographs. Infact, he was honest to the point that he did it with his face appearing. He implored me not to show anybody and all that.....

I was sorry from the profundity of my heart and let him know anything it takes I will make it dependent upon him. He previously kidded about getting him favor and afterward kidded about how he wanted to be gay since he realized I was desolate .

We continued to impart consistently and at some point, he let me know favor told him not to call her and impeded his number. He sounded hurt yet I had a go at encouraging him. Along the line, he let me know he was going for a course and won't be back for some time. I didn't hear from Chukwuma for practically north of a year. He wasn't on any web-based entertainment as he had erased his Twitter account (clearly, over our senseless games on him).

Life went on.

I was returning from midweek administration one day when I got a call. It was chukwuma. In the street I shouted and started to sob. He recently continued to say "eiyahhhh.....You wear truly miss Me" .

He asked where I was and in the event that I could come get him at the air terminal. I immediately got a taxi and went directly to meet him. He had recently landed and I was his most memorable port of call. Adequately abnormal , I petitioned God for him in chapel that very evening.

I flew into his arms once I put complete focus on him and he squashed me with an embrace. He had lost very some weight and looked much more obscure. He inquired as to whether I actually remained alone and in the event that my place was accessible; I said OK.

On our ride back home, he filled me in regarding his excursion , how he had fallen so sick (which made sense of his weight reduction) and how he's chosen to stop the military. He asked after favor and I informed him on her movement to Holland to accompany her better half. All he did was shake his head.

As we returned home, he went kneeling down next to the bed (I went along with him) and expressed appreciation. After that he let me know he was eager. I had soup in the cooler so while I was setting him up dinner, he came into the kitchen and inquired as to whether I currently had a beau. I said no.

"why?" He inquired.

I let him know sweetheart material are scant to find. He giggled loudly and inquired as to whether I had ultimately engaged in sexual relations. I told the truth. I let him know I had-engaged in sexual relations. He asked when last, and I was likewise legitimate. He inquired as to whether I was screwed quite well and I let him in on there was entrance involved...just making out. Furthermore, I didn't even cum.

Chukwuma was so nosey. He needed to hear every one of the subtleties. Indeed, even to how the folks dick was. I could detect a sprinkle of envy in his voice. "Is it enormous like my own?" He inquired.

"how might I know when I have not seen yours at this point?"

"LIAR!!!!" he yelled. "you have seen it on picture jor"

"Am looking at seeing it live" I answered in guard.

"is you that would rather not see it nah...you had the open door however you missed it ."

" you mean the inn ??? Story!!!! With the goal that you will beat me like a hoodlum ba?"

He began snickering so hard to the point I got befuddled.

"so you go stand dey look make man like you dey beat you? You're simply a horrendous non military personnel"

I froze at his remark and quickly he saw my difference in temperament.

"I didn't mean it like that nah....Why taking it personal?....seems you lash out effectively ?" He said.

Meanwhile he was grinning. That was something I'd saw about him. He was continuously grinning. He appeared to be the sort who communicated his feelings (No matter what it was) by grinning alone.

I dished his food, served him and went to sit a long way from him. He continued to apologize yet I didn't respond to him.

He just plunked down actually grinning. He declined eating and his food was getting cold. I was in the middle of taking a gander at my telephone when out of nowhere I took a gander at him and shockingly, Chukwuma was perspiring bountifully. The fan was on, he had showered .... so what was off-base?

"Chukwuma!!!!" I called him out of dread.

Right away, he rushed into the latrine and started to hurl. I needed to rush close to him and rub his back. He was all the while grinning.

Subsequent to cleaning up and flushing his mouth, I helped him to the couch and permitted him to recover. At the point when he did, I took care of him with my own hands. He requested that I get his medicine and I did. Subsequent to taking them , I assisted him to the bed with staying. He started having fever and I got a moist towel to rub him until he works off.

As I laid next to him , he called out to me and I replied. He cuddled dependent upon me and we nestled. His body was so hot however I couldn't have cared less. He had just his briefs on him while I had just a shirt and free fighters. He began letting me know how he has fever and gets sick whenever he's very fomented or stressed. Said the last time he had that impression was the point at which he lost his mum.

His head was on my chest and his arms safely wrapped me.

"do you actually need to wear your shirt?" He said indistinctly. I didn't hold back. As I removed my shirt, he eliminated his briefs and laid ontop of me. He wasn't erect yet I was.

"might you at any point make me discharge ?.....it's been so long....." He murmured. "I've recently been contemplating you....and What Your mouth can Do". I could detect he was grinning as he talked his admissions. I feather touched his strong back and he breathed in noisily yet leisurely. His head was covered on my neck so I started tonguing major areas of strength for him shoulder. I felt the wetness of his lips on my neck and afterward his tongue. My neck isn't delicate but since I realized he wanted some support, I started to groan delicately and move my body gradually under his devastating weight.

His mouth went from my neck to my ears and he started to laugh as he said "I no sabi o.....as in kiss or Do". I realized he was coming clean. Chukwuma was excessively timid and is a generally excellent kid that grew up under extremely severe Christian guardians. He was endeavoring finding a way striking ways to emerge from his shell the time we met on Twitter.

I carried his face to mine and I kissed him. Investigating his lips and tongue with mine. He answered however recently continued grinning which made the kissing meeting a piece off-kilter. I could feel his dick developing on my exposed thighs. Extending in width and length as he started pounding his dick on mine. As I endeavored to eliminate my fighters, he helped me. His kissing turned out to be more serious as well as his frotting.

He moved on his back and I started working my tongue all around every last trace of his body. His dick continued to gesture irately as pre cum leaked out apathetically from his thick rooster cap.

At the point when I got to his dick in the wake of loving his body, I began from licking up the precum that had streamed down his thick shaft. His dick photograph was literally nothing contrasted with reality. As I licked, he wriggled marginally. Be that as it may, when I sucked the dick head like a ravenous child does on a taking care of jug, he yanked his body so hard he wound up sitting up. I took him serenely right down my throat and he groaned like there's no tomorrow. His dick was extremely gigantic and thick that a point, my jaw throbbed so insane that I needed to pull out to knead my jaw. In any case, before I could completely remove my mouth his powerful dick , he got my head and pulled me back to his dick.

Chukwuma held my head down and screwed my mouth like no man's business till it arrived at the point I strongly drove him away out of jaw torment.

He was all the while snickering and grinning. His dick was shinning with my spit as it gestured a "great" to me.

"might I at any point enter you ?"

He asked, more timidly than apprehensively with his eyes still frail from sickness. I grinned back at him and got off the bed to get the essential elements for the cooking meeting.

"do you have hot gasp?" He asked energetically.

I took a gander at him with thrill since I generally fantasize to the contemplations of getting bored by him with my strap since He let me know he had an obsession for clothing when we talked on Twitter.

I had a pristine male G-string In my storeroom and I went to get it. At the point when I put it on, I could see his eyes gleam with want. "So Sweet" he murmured to himself.

He was presently situated at the edge of the bed as he loosened up two strong looking arms coaxing me to come to him. His looks was as though he needed to cry.

Furnished with my condom and lube, I stooped before him and chipped away at his thick chamber molded wood. Condom now fitted and very much lubed up, I sat across his weighty strong thighs and started to kiss him. His huge hands running enthusiastically down my back as his tongue embraced mine. "finger my pussy daddy" I murmured into his ears. What's more, finger me he did.

He pressed and pulled my butt so wide separated to the degree I felt he was determined to destroy me. The more he fingered my butt hole, the more extreme his kisses became. He had extremely lengthy fingers and having 3 of them force their direction into my opening was comparable to getting screwed. My butt was at that point dribbling away it's honey squeeze so I realized it was at that point ready to be slaughtered.

I situated his dick to focus on my opening and gradually I started to sink down on It. Chukwuma held my two ass cheeks and crushed them so particularly hard as he separated them wide enough so they will not slow down the on going entrance.

The entrance appeared to be continuing perpetually and I had previously started feeling so involved in my opening. I needed to put my hand to check how far I had gone with taking his long fat dick just to acknowledge there was even more dick I was at this point to take. I surrendered as I said "I can't" to him.

My butt hole was at that point taking steps to tear, my stomach was stacked with dick...still there was more dick to take????? . "It is unimaginable" I finished up.

"take a gander at me....look at me" Chukwuma said as he took my face in his huge hands.

"you can do it baby....you can take it....don't be afraid....Just make up your mind....baby???....look at me....don't stop.."

He energized.

I took a gander at him and maybe I was seeing him interestingly. I saw everything about variety his eyes held. He was so lovely. He grinned from his eyes and I knew for specific it came from his spirit. I grinned back and kissed him. With a yell of win like a champion in fight , I gave one last push

I started holding unto to Chukwuma firmly for my dear life as rushes of agony and delight overwhelmed my faculties. I dug my nails into the tissue on his back and spot his shoulder hard. Chukwuma didn't actually wince to the aggravation and injury I was causing for him.

"indeed baby.....you made it....you got it done" his huge hands started stroking my head the manner in which moms do to their crying children while soothing them.

I was moaning and groaning as he continued petting me saying "it's okay". Following couple of moments, he started to tenderly push. Our brow together as we both grinned while investigating each other's eyes. With his body actually igniting with fever, his muscle strong chest and pointed areolas jabbing my skin, his enormous solid hands crushing and stroking me everywhere, his larger than usual penis pushing inside me, I felt like I was in paradise. I started to return his push which uttered our crash extremely wet and slurpy.

The more he screwed me, the harder I bobbed on his weighty post condemning all wariness and results that might happen to my butt.

He laid me on the floor and mounted me. To say he beat me like sweet potato is putting it mildly. I asked for it....infact I sobbed tears of glad happiness. I could feel the condom tear cos the erosion turned out to be excessively sweet and excessively crude. I accepted Chukwuma knew additionally cos his groans turned out to be so exceptionally clearly as his push sped up.

Quickly he came over me as he groaned "take it baby....please take it....ooooohhhhhhh take It " I opened my mouth as planes of thick sperm offloaded into my eager mouth. His cum poured like a water fall and I gulped all of it and sucked it a more to guarantee none was hidding. He groaned and shuddered as I sucked him until he went delicate.

We laid in one another's arms...too powerless to get up, tidy up or get on the bed. We wound up dozing on the floor.

Around midnight, I felt his finger in my opening. He probably spat on his hands cos when his fingers were wet. He focused on spit my opening and when I started to fight that he stops, he murmured he won't screw me yet simply needed to rest soundly.

Gradually I felt his chicken sliding into my opening. It didn't feel difficult May be on the grounds that I was as yet opened. When he was inside me, he held me close and said "great night child."

My poop hole started to throb on his dick and he started to chuckle. "assuming you proceed with I go screw you o!" I promptly let him know I wasn't doing it deliberately that it was compulsory activity.

For reasons unknown, my poop hole wouldn't quit jerking on his fat weighty rooster. He started to answer every throb with a push. "I have zero control over myself o" he said. I was too feeble to even think about dissenting so I just permitted myself float to rest.

I started to dream Chukwuma was fucking me in a delightful nursery that was essential for our home. We had quite recently hitched and our visitor where hanging tight for us to come and cut the wedding cake. I was beseeching him to stop since I didn't believe my cum should over-indulge my outfit however he didn't stop. I could feel my cum coming so Out of dread in my fantasy, I out of nowhere awakened exclusively to find Chukwuma fucking me so great And wanking me simultaneously. Before I could recover cognizance, sperm was spilling out of my dick in huge amount.

My butt hole felt so sore and I was in torment. I had a go at eliminating myself from Chukwuma's hug however at that point he grasped me wildly and began to screw me with such an excess of energy that I shouted and beseeched him to stop. His enormous hard covered my mouth right away and he expanded his beat. I figured I will kick the bucket on the off chance that he didn't stop. "it's coming baby....it's coming......it's coooooommmmmiiiiinnnngggggg aaahhhhhhssshhhhhhhh!!!!!!" he groaned as slugs of hot sperm shot my poop hole like an assault rifle.

I was in tears.

"Am sorry baby....forgive me...... you're too sweet....I couldn't avoid You....you know it's my first time....sorry" he asked as he petted me.

He Still had his dick inside me as he continued to pet me. Gradually I floated to rest.

Toward the beginning of the day , I left for work while Chukwuma was all the while resting on the floor wheezing vigorously. He was exposed. His colossal body and dozing situated made him seem to be a Greek god. I snapped a picture of him and afterward concealed him while putting a cushion under his head. I additionally saw his temperature had returned to typical.

I got to work limping. My partners asked me what occurred and I let them know I had a mishap. While at work, Chukwuma called me to check in the event that I was okay. I let him know I will be OK. At the point when I asked how he was doing, he said he's been having erection the entire day and inquired as to whether it was ordinary since he's never had such erectile issues. I let him know I couldn't really understand.

My manager at work saw how I limped and requested that I go home for the day. I knew whether I returned home, Chukwuma will need to screw me so I called him and asked he take a taxi and meet me at the ocean side (which is near my work environment).

Minutes after the fact he showed up. Wearing shorts and a white shirt. As he strolled towards me, my heart summersaulted on different occasions. This person was a divine being. He started to grin again once he saw me. "what is wrong? This one you dey look me like TV" he asked me. He embraced me and asked how I was doing and apologized for the previous evening. I got some information about his wellbeing and he said he felt quite a bit improved. He presently came to my ear and sang a line from Marvin Gaye's tune (sexual recuperating). He sang-"Your sexual recuperating is something really great for me." He snickered and drove him away.

As we went for a stroll, he halted at a seller and got us drink and roll. Directly before individuals, he proposed to take care of me. I was bashful and needed to reject yet from the thoroughly search in his eyes (his grinned disappeared out of nowhere) , I realized I dare not endeavor denying. I tasted from the straw of his viju drink and as I Did, his grin returned.

"right". He said proudly

A man who was purchasing cigarette close to us saw what was happening and presently said - "we no dey do that kain tin here o....make una convey una grimy life smell out from here."

Before I could squint, Chukwuma plunged on this man and ruined him. It took more than 5 men to have the option to eliminate him from the unfortunate man.

The man was draining from his mouth and nose. He needed to begin yelling "homo" yet before the words left his mouth, Chukuma streaked his ID. I thought he was a normal trooper yet the way that off-base I was. He was a high positioned official. Turned out one more warrior was there in the group and Chukwuma provided him orders to train him.

I plunked down drinking my viju with my hero as I watched the unfortunate man getting embarrassed. Everyone came to beseech us to let the man go however Chukwuma was unyielding. He didn't act like anyone was conversing with him.

Not many days after the fact, he left for Zaria. He let me know the legislative issues happening in the military was excessively. I had a go at persuading him to not leave however all he said was that he will consider it.

I couldn't say whether I will call him my beau or not however one thing am certain about is that he is totally into me. On two events he's demonstrated insane love. One was the point at which he passed on Zaria around midnight to ensure he was with me during my supplement activity (which was extremely off the cuff) . The subsequent time was that he had an authority capability somewhere near Lagos state and I let him know I was so horny for him. He left his task and came to screw me. He got trained for his activities at work yet said he couldn't have cared less.